I BELIEVE
in the
HOLY GHOST

Maynard James

Foreword by Norman Grubb

OLIPHANTS

OLIPHANTS

BLUNDELL HOUSE

GOODWOOD ROAD

LONDON S.E.14

© Bethany Fellowship, Inc. 1965

First British Edition 1969

SBN 551 00355 3

*Printed in Great Britain by
Redwood Press Limited, Trowbridge, Wilts.*

Foreword

I HAVE BEEN TREADING on holy ground as I have read this manuscript.

It is in response to the request of my old friend and beloved brother in Christ, Maynard James, that I write this foreword. I have often heard Maynard preach, and I know him to be a God-inspired prophet of a full salvation. But not till reading this manuscript did I realize that he is also a Biblical scholar.

The range and aptness of his Biblical references, the breadth and scope of his quotations from theological authors through the centuries, and the pungency of his facts and illustrations collected from all kinds of sources, grip my attention. I must confess that I read enough Biblical publications to quickly lose interest when the presentation is not beyond the ordinary. But this manuscript has held my interest.

Way beyond that, however, there is an atmosphere in what Maynard James here writes. It reminds me of the title of Rudolph Otto's classic, *The Idea of the Holy*. This is entering into the holiest—the Holy Spirit speaking by man on the Holy Spirit.

It is not a light book. It is not a bunch of diverting illustrations to capture the ephemeral interest of a quiet afternoon. It is not that modern atrocity that masquerades as a living book—a series of sermons! It is a serious presentation for serious readers on that most serious of all subjects—God the Spirit. But it is written in no dead fashion of the theological treatise;

it is with the same fire burning through its pages as burns in the author's preaching, and with the same depth of concern to see the Holy Spirit outpoured on the Church today as at Pentecost, and through the Church to the world.

The Holy Spirit at Pentecost is the Holy Spirit of today. He is at work, and the promise is to every believer: "He that believeth on me, . . . from within him shall flow rivers of living water. But this spake he of the Spirit."

> Norman P. Grubb
> International Secretary
> The Worldwide Evangelization Crusade

Contents

Preface

THIS BOOK is not purposefully controversial. That does not mean that nobody will dispute certain statements in it concerning the operation of the Holy Spirit in human experience. In fact, the new penetration of the so-called Charismatic Movement has aroused fierce debate all over the Christian world. And what book on the Holy Spirit is complete that does not honestly face the important issue of the gifts of the Spirit?

The author has earnestly sought to set forth those truths about the Paraclete which have burned themselves into his own heart. To "score points" against any Christians who may differ from him in their interpretation of the baptism of the Holy Spirit is the last thing he desires. In the course of his travels in various parts of the world he has constantly met Christians from different denominations who were hungry in heart for a Spirit-filled experience—a life of joy and victory in the Holy Ghost. If, through the reading of this little volume, some fellow believers in Christ are led into a satisfying experience of full salvation, the author will be amply rewarded.

Sincere thanks are given to the Nazarene Publishing House for permission to republish chapter 16, which the author first wrote in *The Holiness Pulpit*, compiled by James McGraw.

M. G. J.

Southport, Lancashire, 1964

CHAPTER ONE

The Sin of Neglect

HARDENING OF THE ARTERIES is a dangerous sign. It tells of abnormal blocking of the coronary blood vessels. It speaks of decaying strength.

Not long ago I heard a prominent evangelical leader make a timely and courageous confession. He publicly lamented that his beloved denomination (barely sixty years old) was already suffering from "hardening of the arteries." Such a confession came as a necessary shock to any listeners who were content to assess spiritual progress in terms of finance and academic finesse.

But why hardening of the arteries in a young society whose doctrines are Scriptural and whose Manual standards are high?

The answer is plain. It is because the Holy Spirit is not having full sway in the lives of its members. For the Holy Spirit never grows old. He is "the Eternal Spirit" (Heb. 9:14). He is never weary. His resources are inexhaustible. And when a Christian is completely possessed by Him who has been termed "the Executive of the Godhead," then he is continually "strengthened with might by his Spirit in the inner man" (Eph. 3:16).

Paul's happy confession was this: "But though our
outward man perish, yet the inward man is renewed
day by day" (II Cor. 4:16).

There is fulfilled in the experience of the Spirit-
filled Christian the gracious promise to the patriarch
Asher: "And as thy days, so shall thy strength be."

It is a major tragedy that for many years so-called
evangelical believers in Christ have failed to honor
the Holy Ghost. Lip service has taken the place of
loving obedience and implicit trust. The ardent worship of the Comforter has been neglected. In its place
has come the click of ecclesiastical machinery and the
pressure of denominational programs.

It is imperative, in this dark hour of history, that
the Church of Jesus gets back to Pentecost. Or to put
it more correctly, that she receives that final outpouring of the Holy Spirit which is promised "before the
great and terrible day of the Lord come" (Joel 3:28–
31).

"The Acts chapter two Pentecost" was a partial fulfillment of Joel's great prophecy. Its completion is yet
to come. The last outpouring of the Holy Ghost will
be on the eve of God's world-wide judgments upon
apostate sinners.

Let there be no mistake about it: another Pentecost
would mean a return to apostolic Christianity, with its
glorious signs and wonders and miracles (Heb. 3:4).
It would, as it were, write more pages to the Acts
of the Apostles. Yes, and it would bring a fresh unveiling of Jesus Christ as the risen and almighty
Saviour—One who is alive for evermore. For it is the
special delight of the Holy Ghost to reveal and exalt
the person of Jesus. Not only so: it is also the work
of the Spirit to make sinners into saints—to transform
them into the likeness of Christ. For it is through the
operation of the Holy Ghost that Christians "beholding

the glory of the Lord, are changed into the same image from glory to glory" (II Cor. 3:18). Mark the crescendo here: "from glory to glory." Surely this shows no sign of spiritual decay! In fact, there can be no "hardening of the arteries" when the Spirit of Him who raised up Christ from the dead is reigning in our mortal bodies.

It is God's intense desire that His church should be "as fair as the moon, clear as the sun, and terrible as an army with banners" (Song of Sol. 6:10).

The great mystery is why the Church of Christ has so neglected the Holy Spirit down the centuries. That this terrible sin has been committed is beyond dispute. The records of church history are damning in their exposure of the shameful treatment of the Holy Spirit by God's people. Like Jesus, the Holy Spirit has been "wounded in the house of his friends."

Quite a few years ago a certain chorus was sung in many churches. It ran something like this:

> "Glory, glory to God,
> My heart is now cleansed from sin;
> I've abandoned myself to the Holy Ghost,
> And His fulness abides within."

We sang it in Cliff College in the days of Samuel Chadwick. That great man of God liked it, not because of the tune to which the chorus was sung, but because of the words, "I've abandoned myself to the Holy Ghost."

I wonder how many Christians today could sing from their hearts, "I've *abandoned* myself to the Holy Ghost, And His fulness abides within"?

We plead for a return to apostolic Christianity. It is our only hope.

Bitter controversy has assailed the modern Pente-

costal Movement. That some of its most determined
opponents, as well as its best friends, have come alike
from evangelical, Bible-loving circles is a mystery
which one day will be solved. Meanwhile we must
wait with patience for God's own explanation.

One thing is clear, however. Out of the heat and
dust of battle has emerged this compensating factor:
the Pentecostal Movement of the past five or six decades has drawn more attention to the character and
ministry of the Holy Spirit than any other religious
society has done for centuries. And for this we should
be deeply thankful. For since the passing of the first
few generations of Christianity, no doctrine of the
Christian faith has been so neglected as that of the
Holy Spirit.

That the Apostles' Creed contains ten articles on
the Person and work of Christ, but only one on the
Holy Spirit, is singular indeed. Passing strange, also,
is the comparative silence of the Greek and Roman
Church Fathers on the operations of the Holy Ghost
in relation to man. In fact, as Dr. George Smeaton
has observed, the period of the Reformation (16th
century) gave a testimony to the Holy Spirit more
full and explicit than had ever been uttered since the
apostolic age.[1] Writing in our own day, Samuel Chadwick declared that no great book on the Holy Spirit
had been written since 1674,[2] when the illustrious
John Owen, Nonconformist Vice-Chancellor of Oxford,
produced his notable work: *Concerning the Holy Spirit*.

Even in 1963, such an authoritative treatise as the
Encyclopaedia Britannica showed a strange dis-
proportion when it came to the important theme of the
Holy Spirit. Quite recently, when searching in the 1957
edition, I found to my surprise that while over 32 pages
were entirely devoted to the papacy, less than three
pages were given to the subject of the Holy Spirit!

It should be stated, however, at this point, that the hymns of the Christian Church have occasionally helped to fill a little of the gap left by the theologians regarding the Paraclete. Take, for example, the well-known Latin hymn of the 9th century, translated by Bishop Cosin. It begins:

> Come, Holy Ghost, our souls inspire
> And lighten with celestial fire;
> Thou the anointing Spirit art,
> Who dost Thy sevenfold gifts impart.

But all too rare have been such canticles on the Spirit. The silence of the centuries has been tragic indeed.

This sad neglect of the Holy Spirit by the Christian Church is all the more remarkable when we remember the importance and prominence of the theme. John Owen spoke of the doctrine of the Holy Spirit as the touchstone of faith; the one article by which the Church stands or falls. Samuel Chadwick said that the Holy Spirit is the ultimate fact of revelation and the unique force in redemption.

It has been pointed out that the Holy Spirit is directly mentioned not less than 86 times in the Old Testament and at least 261 times in the New Testament. Some Christians would be quite surprised if told that 25 different names or titles are given to the Holy Spirit in the Scriptures. At a Bible quiz it would be interesting to find out how many could recite from memory more than six or seven of these titles.

It might prove our point if, in passing, we mentioned just twelve of the names given to the Spirit of God:

1. The Spirit of Holiness—Romans 1:4.
2. The Eternal Spirit—Hebrews 9:14.
3. The Spirit of Christ—Romans 8:9.

4. The Spirit of Life—Romans 8:2.
5. The Spirit of Truth—John 14:1, 17.
6. The Holy Ghost—Matthew 1:18.
7. The Spirit of Grace—Hebrews 10:29.
8. The Spirit of Adoption—Romans 8:15.
9. The Promise of the Father—Acts 1:4.
10. The Comforter—John 14:26.
11. The Spirit of Glory—I Peter 4:14.
12. The Spirit of Counsel and Might—Isaiah 11:2.

With what tender awe and reverence should we stand before the Third Person of the adorable Trinity! He is the Eternal Spirit who in II Corinthians 3:18 (ASV) is called, "The Lord the Spirit."

If to blaspheme against Him is the unpardonable sin, then indeed He is a person of supreme importance.

Jesus told us plainly that the Holy Spirit is He who speaks, guides, teaches, reveals and convicts (John 14–16). The Apostle Paul said that the Spirit could be grieved and quenched (Eph. 4:30; I Thess. 5:19), and Saint Peter declared that professing Christians could "tempt" the Holy Ghost and even lie to Him (Acts 5:3, 9).

Every child of God is commanded to be filled with the Spirit and to walk in the Spirit (Eph. 5:18; Gal. 5:16).

In succeeding chapters we shall contemplate at least four matchless operations of the Holy Spirit throughout those ages which have a direct bearing upon the affairs of this earth. They are (1) in creation; (2) in the formation of the written Word—the Bible; (3) in relation to the Incarnate Word—the Lord Jesus Christ; (4) in and upon the human heart.

---

1 *The Doctrine of the Holy Spirit*, p. 367
2 *The Way of Pentecost*, p. 9

CHAPTER TWO

The Holy Spirit in Creation

"AND THE SPIRIT OF GOD moved upon the face of the waters" (Gen. 1:2).

Standing infinitely high above all the creation myths of the ancient pagan world is the Bible account of the beginning of the universe. Free from absurdly fantastic embellishments, it tells in plain language of a marvellous creation from nothing by the eternal God.

"In the beginning God created the heavens and the earth" (Gen. 1:1).

"For by him were all things created, that are in heaven, or that are in earth, visible and invisible... all things were created by him and for him" (Col. 1:16).

Since God is uncreated, there must have been a time when there was no universe. There were no stars, no worlds, no angels—nothing but God himself. The puny mind of fallen man cannot grasp this awe-inspiring fact. It reels at the thought of a God without a beginning, a God who at one time was unrelated to anything but himself.

Rejecting the sublime Biblical revelation of an eternal God, man's darkened reason has sometimes conjured up the idea of an uncreated, eternal existence of the universe and of matter. But, as Erich Sauer has reminded us, if we are to accept a beginning and a creation of the world, a belief in a personal, living, almighty God is necessary.[1] Indeed, scientists are finding it increasingly difficult to believe in the eternity of matter. Even in the disintegration of radio-active substances modern science has produced further evidence that the universe had a beginning.

Professor Karl Heim, the eminent mathematician, scientist and theologian, has put it this way: "The daring dreams of the philosophers that the universe is eternal has today—even purely from the scientific point of view—become improbable."

Bishop Stephen Neil believes that the greatest act of God's self-emptying was the creation of a universe on which He would confer existence in a measure independent of himself.[2] We cannot go all the way with Neil in this assertion, but one thing is clear: the creation of the universe stands out as a glorious manifestation of God's love, humility and power.

In that wondrous act of creation the triune God was engaged. The unity of the Deity was conclusive when the universe was formed.

As the great John Owen emphasized: "Every person is the author of every work of God, because each person is God, and the divine nature is the same undivided principle of all the divine operations."[3] Thus John Wesley wrote: "We have the fullest evidence that the eternal, omnipresent, almighty, all-wise Spirit, as He created all things, so He continually superintends what He has created." [4]

The Bible tells of the vital part played by the Holy Spirit in creation.

In Job 26:13 we read: "By his Spirit he hath garnished the heavens."

Elihu exclaimed: "The Spirit of God hath made

me" (Job 33:4).

In Psalm 104:30, David declared: "Thou sendest forth thy Spirit, they are created: and thou renewest the face of the earth."

That lovely 10th-century hymn on the Holy Spirit, translated by John Dryden, begins aptly:

> "Creator Spirit; by whose aid
> The world's foundations first were laid."

But it is over Genesis 1:2 that Christian sages and scientists have pondered most. It reads: "And the earth was without form, and void; and darkness was upon the face of the deep. And the Spirit of God moved upon the face of the waters."

There is a view, held by many Bible scholars and scientists, whose roots go back in Christian literature even to the time of Augustine (C. 400).

It is known as the Restitution Theory. It holds that the primeval chaos and darkness of Genesis 1:2 was the result of a great catastrophe, in which Satan rebelled against God. The earth, which had been created by God without blemish, became, in consequence of satanic revolt, a black ruin, enveloped by waste waters. Thus between verses 1 and 2 of Genesis chapter 1, there may be a gap of millions of years.

This gap, claim the Restitutionists, makes full allowance for the so-called prehistoric geological periods. Says General von Viehbahn, the well-known German preacher: "A new creation was necessary before man, created in the image of God, was appointed to be ruler upon the earth. After this had taken place, 'God saw everything that he had made, and behold, it was very good.'"

In other words, this means that the work of the six days in Genesis 1:3–31 was not the original creation of the world itself, but a work of restoration.

The question is asked: Is it not unthinkable that a dark, waste and empty world should have issued immediately from the creative hand of the God of light, order, and fulness of life?

Does not Isaiah 45:18 tell us that God did *not* create the world a waste (*tohu*: the same word occurs in Genesis 1:2)? Rather did He form it to be inhabited.

A further question arises: How could the hosts of heaven have rejoiced and shouted for joy at the foundation of this earth, if this creation had at the first been desolate and chaotic?

Did not God himself say to Job, "Where wast thou when I laid the foundations of the earth? Who laid the corner stone thereof; when the morning stars sang together, and all the sons of God shouted for joy?" (Job 38:4, 6, 7).

It is also claimed by the advocates of the Restitution theory, that the words, "And the earth was without form, and void," (*tohu-wa-bohu*) could be rendered, consistently with Hebrew idiom: "Now the earth *had become* waste and void." They point out that the Hebrew verb *hayah*, used in Genesis 1:2, often has the meaning, "to become," e.g. Psalm 118:22, "The stone which the builders rejected *is become* the head of the corner."

Of course, it is only fair to state that there are equally devout and skillful theologians and scientists who do not agree with the Restitutionists in their interpretation of Genesis chapter 1. Space does not permit us to discuss the arguments of those who hold the "Period" theory of creation. Ruling out the idea of a "gap" between verses 1 and 2 of Genesis 1, they believe that "the astonishing coincidence of the scientific order and of the Biblical order of creation seems to indicate that the Biblical days (of Genesis chapter 1) correspond to periods of geological time."—Prof. Rendle Short. This simply means that we cannot literally interpret the days of creation as days of 24 hours.

Advocates in both schools (Restitution and Period) are firm believers in the plenary inspiration of the original Scriptures.

Whatever view is held, one truth stands out like a Mount Everest. It is that only the sublime operations of the Holy Spirit could have transformed a scene of blackness, death, formlessness and ruin into a panorama of light, life, order and beauty.

"And the Spirit of God moved upon the face of the waters. And God said, Let there be light: and there was light."

Satan may have wrought fearful havoc when he rebelled against God. Chaos beyond remedy and darkness defying penetration seemed to have afflicted this earth when Lucifer fell. But what terror must have seized Satan and his legions when they knew that God the Holy Spirit had arrived on the scene of devastation!

The Almighty could be disobeyed and deeply grieved. But He could never be defeated. So, "brooding" with His creative energies over the face of the dark waters, the blessed Holy Spirit wrought surpassing triumph over all that was alien to the divine will. When His work had ended, there stood forth God's masterpiece—man, inbreathed by the Holy Spirit, made in the likeness of His Creator, and anointed to be king over the earth.

In the creative work of the Spirit in Genesis 1 are seen the three canons of art: viz., light, form and beauty.

A few years ago an eye specialist in Kenya told me an unusual story. He once visited a private exhibition of paintings in South Africa. Impressed by the radiant beauty and symmetry of the pictures, he expressed his admiration to a bystander, who happened to be the artist himself. The exhibitor then told my friend the secret of his paintings. He said that becoming a real Christian had revolutionized his paintings. No longer bound to any modern surrealist conception of art, he was inspired to paint according to God's own pattern— paintings full of light, form and beauty. He confessed, however, that at a certain art conference he attended, his own Christian conception of art was distinctly frowned upon by his fellow painters.

It is strangely true that men still "love darkness rather than light." Only the Holy Spirit can dispel the gloom.

Standing over the chaos and darkness that envelops most of our earth today is the Holy Spirit, ready to manifest His wondrous creative power. But He patiently waits for ruined men to call upon Him for deliverance and new life.

His great delight is to chase away the darkness of *sin*, to re-create the sinner in the image of Jesus Christ, and to infuse His own life into the dead. Yes, and to make the human heart His abode. To redeemed sinners Paul could write: "Know ye not that your body is the temple of the Holy Ghost which is in you?" (I Cor. 6:19).

> "Life-giving Spirit, o'er us move,
>   As on the formless deep;
> Give life and order, light and love,
>   Where now is death or sleep."

---

1 *The King of the Earth*, p. 203
2 *Christian Faith and Other Faiths*, p. 13
3 *Concerning the Holy Spirit*, pp. 96 ff.
4 Sermon CXIX on the Unity of the Divine Being

CHAPTER THREE

The Holy Spirit and the Bible

THE BIBLE is the special creation of the Holy Spirit. Written by about forty persons over a period of some 1,600 years, its author is none other than the Third Person of the Trinity.

No one knows this better than Satan himself; hence his fury against the Word of God, which is the "sword of the Spirit." [1] Ceaselessly he endeavors to discredit and undermine the authority of the Scriptures.

It was the written Word that Jesus used in defeating the wiles of the devil in the Wilderness of Temptation. Three times the Master quoted, not from the Greek philosophers, but from the book of Deuteronomy. It was this two-edged sword that pierced the armor of the Wicked One and put him to flight. To this very day Satan flees before the Word of God when uttered in the power of the Holy Ghost.

That the Scriptures have a supernatural influence in transforming incorrigible sinners into eminent saints is beyond cavil. The authentic reports of the British and Foreign Bible Society and the various missionary societies are sufficient proof of this.

An up-to-date illustration is the case of the Rev. David Sol, who for over twenty years has been a district superintendent of the Church of the Nazarene in southeast Mexico.

His own conversion to Christ was a miracle. Someone carried a Bible, wrapped in a piece of brown paper, across the mountain, and it reached David Sol, who then was a very wicked young man. Simply by reading God's Word, and without any human aid, David Sol was gloriously saved. For seven years he was pastor of a church in his own home town of Villa Flores, and from this town have come twenty-three preachers of the Gospel!

Such instances of the miraculous power of the Scriptures could be multiplied a hundredfold.

The tragedy of our day is that Satan no longer needs the help of non-Christian philosophers like Porphyry and Spinoza in attacking the plenary inspiration of the original Scriptures. He now has an army of so-called Christian Bible scholars to do his deadly work.

The Christian Church has always believed that in a special manner the writers of the Scriptures had been inspired by the Holy Spirit for the purpose of revealing to mankind the divine plan of salvation, and to give the Church the principles it needed for guidance.

The Westminster Confession states that "the supreme Judge, by whom all controversies of religion are determined, and all decrees of councils ... can be no other but the Holy Spirit speaking in Scripture." [2]

The learned Samuel Horsley (1733–1806), Bishop of St. Asaph, referring to the writers of Scripture, declared: "You will perhaps think it incredible that they, who were assisted by the divine Spirit when they preached, should be deserted by that Spirit when they committed what they preached to writing. ... You will think it unlikely that they, who were led by the Spirit into all truth, should be permitted to lead the whole Church for many ages into error."

The apostles Peter and Paul, along with the Psalmist David, were convinced that the Holy Ghost was the Author of the Scriptures. Here are their clear statements on this vital matter:

Peter: "No prophecy of the scripture is of any private interpretation. For the prophecy came not at any time by the will of man: but holy men of God spake as they were moved [borne along] by the Holy Ghost" (II Pet. 1:20, 21, marg.).

". . . this scripture must needs have been fulfilled, which the Holy Ghost by the mouth of David spake before concerning Judas" (Acts 1:16).

David: "The spirit of the Lord spake by me, and his word was in my tongue" (II Sam. 23:2).

Paul: "Well spake the Holy Ghost by Esaias the prophet unto our fathers, saying, Go unto this people, and say, Hearing ye shall hear, and shall not understand; and seeing ye shall see, and not perceive" (Acts 28:25, 26).

Here Paul is quoting from Isaiah, chapter six, and says it was the word of the Holy Ghost himself through the prophet.

"All scripture is given by inspiration of God, and is profitable for doctrine, for reproof, for correction, for instruction in righteousness" (II Tim. 3:16).

It is interesting to notice that the Greek word used by Paul for "inspiration of God" is *theopneustos*. This word really means "God-breathed," and proves that it was the "Breath" of God, the Holy Spirit himself, who caused the Scriptures to be given.

Most important of all is the testimony of *Jesus Christ* concerning the Scriptures. Citing the Old Testament passage, Psalm 110:1, our Lord said unto the Pharisees, "How is it then that David, inspired by the

Spirit, calls him Lord?" (Matt. 22:43, ASV).

That this Old Testament Scripture, like every other Bible passage, shares the prerogative of inviolability is made clear by Jesus in His words to the unbelieving Jews: "The scripture cannot be broken" (John 10:35).

In view of such authentic statements concerning the divine authorship of the Bible, how distressing are some of the dogmatic utterances of many modern theologians. Two examples must suffice:

Professor H. H. Rowley, in his work, *The Book of Daniel*, concludes that "Darius the Mede is a conflation of confused traditions" (page 54). With such a sweeping assertion we entirely disagree. Evidently our Lord placed complete reliance on the writings of Daniel, for He referred to the certainty of that prophet's prediction of the coming Tribulation, and called for a careful observation of Daniel's words.[4]

In his book *The Authority of the Bible* (page 15), Professor C. H. Dodd says, concerning the Book of the Revelation, "A book which, on the whole, is sub-Christian in tone and outlook." Yet this is the book in which the Lamb of God, Christ Jesus, is specially prominent. The title "The Lamb" occurs not less than 28 times in this final part of Scripture.

The writer, the apostle John, says of this book that it was "the revelation of Jesus Christ, which God gave unto him, to shew unto his servants things which must shortly come to pass; and he sent and signified it by his angel unto his servant John: who bare record of the word of God, and of the testimony of Jesus Christ" (Rev. 1:1, 2). Could any writing have a more sacred imprimatur than that? Yet it seems that while Professor Dodd would not accuse the apostle John of deliberate deceit, he feels that sometimes he is under a delusion!

John, however, is sure of his ground. Not only does he clearly state that he was inspired of the Holy Ghost when he received the heavenly visions; he repeatedly exhorts the churches in Asia to hear the voice of the Holy Spirit through these revelations.[5] Finally, as a solemn warning to those who would tamper with the book he had been inspired to write, he declares: "I testify unto every man that heareth the words of the prophecy of this book, If any man shall add unto these things, God shall add unto him the plagues that are written in this book: and if any man shall take away from the words of the book of this prophecy, God shall take away his part out of the book of life." [6]

I prefer to believe that the Holy Spirit inspired John to write the whole of the Book of the Revelation. We can rely upon Him to give His own reply to those who, in their so-called enlightened reasoning, deny the plain words of holy men of God, who wrote as they were carried along by the Holy Spirit. Time is on our side: apocalyptic rumblings are getting louder as the days pass. The spectre of the hydrogen bomb surely underlines the warnings of inspired revelation!

It is obvious to those who have eyes to see, that Satan seeks in these "latter days" to undermine the authority of Scripture by a subtle twofold method:

First: by granting that the Bible is inspired, but taking away the essentially distinctive character of that inspiration.

Second: by denying plenary inspiration on the ground of internal unworthiness in the fabric of the documents.

We evangelicals believe in the plenary inspiration of the original Scriptures. By that we do not mean a stiff, mechanical dictation from God to man in which the human personality was suppressed. We know, of course, that in the Ten Commandments there was divine inscription, and in some parts of Exodus, Leviticus, and Revelation, et cetera, there would appear to be divine dictation. But verbal inspiration explains such cases as being consistent with human freedom. Plenary inspiration contends that the original Scriptures were the result of the inbreathing of God's Holy Spirit into men, qualifying them to receive and communicate divine truth without error. The individuality of the writers was safeguarded, yet infallibility of communication was assured.

We definitely reject Karl Barth's neo-orthodoxy in regard to the Bible. As a force against extreme liberalism it has failed to satisfy the heart and mind of the devout seeker after divine truth. To Karl Barth the Bible is a mixture of truth and legend. He regards only that as the Word of God which the Holy Spirit impresses upon the human mind as such. This means that some parts of the Scriptures are divorced from the Spirit. According to Barth, He, the Paraclete, is not the author of the whole of the Bible.

We ask the question: How can we have an authentic revelation of the historic figures of the past apart from authentic documents? How do we know that Moses, Abraham, and David lived, apart from reliable documentary evidence? Once we start slicing off portions of the Bible as being untrustworthy, we take a big step toward the total displacement of the authority of the Scriptures.

That there are problems arising from implicit faith in the full inspiration of the Scriptures no sensible Bible student would deny. But with Augustine we say: "If here or there I stumble upon something which seems not to agree with the truth, I make no doubt that either the copy is faulty, or the translator did not express exactly the thought of the original, or that I do not understand the matter." In any case, as Erich Sauer puts it, "faith can wait." [7]

It is true that the original Bible manuscripts are

lost. It is also true that God has suffered the introduction of certain faults in the *copying* of the sacred text. And because of this has arisen a widespread objection to belief in plenary inspiration.

Certainly, comparison of hundreds of existing manuscripts of the Old Testament (they are transmissions) reveal many variations in the text. But, as has been shown, many of these variations are only different orthography or older forms of the endings of the same Hebrew words. Regarding the New Testament, it has been pointed out by Dr. F. J. A. Hort, one of the greatest authorities in the field of New Testament textual criticism, that "the proportion of words virtually accepted on all hands as raised above doubt is no less than seven-eighths of the whole. The remaining eighth, therefore, formed in great part by changes of order or other comparative trivialities, constitutes the whole area of criticism." Of this remaining eighth part, it has been said by no less an authority than Dr. W. B. Warfield that ninety-five percent of these variations in the New Testament text "have so little support that their adoption or rejection would cause no appreciable difference in the sense of the passage in which they occur."

It is comforting to read the words of Sir Frederick G. Kenyon in his book *The Bible and Archæology* (p. 228): "The authenticity and the general integrity of the books of the New Testament may be regarded as finally established. . . . The Christian can take the whole Bible in his hand and say without fear or hesitation that he holds in it the true Word of God, handed down without essential loss from generation to generation throughout the centuries." It is of further satisfaction to know that Professor F. F. Bruce regards Sir Frederick Kenyon as being a leading specialist on New Testament textual criticism.

We cannot close this chapter, however, without referring to what may have puzzled many earnest Bible students, the fact that the New Testament writers, when quoting the Old Testament, do not always repeat verbally the Hebrew text. Examples of this are: Hebrews 10:5 with Psalm 40:6; Acts 15:16 with Amos 9:11, 12; and Hebrews 15:5 with Deuteronomy 31:6.

This can be explained if we believe that the uniform author of the whole Bible is the Holy Spirit. For as one eminent Bible scholar has said: "An author has the right to repeat his own statements in freer form, without being compelled to retain their exact wording. Moreover he has the right to make a statement which may follow closely the contents of a former statement but which, to suit some new situation, contains variations. Now when quoting the Old Testament, Christ and the Holy Spirit were taking words out of His own Book (I Pet. 1:11; II Pet. 1:21; Heb. 3:7)."

And so we rest our confidence in the Holy Spirit who gave such glorious revelations to men and who has jealously guarded the sacred canon down the ages. That God should so inspire His prophets to accurately foretell in detail important historical events hundreds and even thousands of years ahead is certain proof of the infallibility of holy Scripture.

Who but the Holy Spirit could and would give a humble fisherman like Peter such an amazing insight into the principles underlying matter, and of the final destruction of the universe, as is briefly outlined in II Peter, chapter three? Why, the scientific language of the apostle challenges any nuclear scientist to describe the same things with equal accuracy and vividness in such few words. Real scientists no longer scoff at Peter's inspired prediction of the final dissolution of the world by atomic forces. Instead they tremble at the staggering accuracy of his words.

Thus, in reverential faith we plead:

> "Come, Holy Ghost, for moved by Thee
>   The prophets wrote and spoke;
> Unlock the truth, Thyself the key,
>   Unseal the sacred Book."

---

1 Ephesians 6:17
2 Ephesians 1:10
3 Tracts (Sermon on the Incarnation), pp. 367 ff.
4 Matthew 24:15
5 Revelation 1:10; 2:7 ff.
6 Revelation 22:18, 19
7 Erich Sauer, *From Eternity to Eternity*, p. 104

CHAPTER FOUR

The Holy Spirit and the Incarnate Word

SIGNIFICANTLY THE NEW TESTAMENT refers to the Holy Ghost as "the Spirit of his Son" and "the Spirit of Christ." [1] This points to the special and intimate relationship between the Holy Spirit and the Lord Jesus in His humanity, public ministry, atonement, and resurrection glory. When our Lord united to himself human nature ("the Word became flesh"), the Holy Spirit was the Cause of the absolute union in Christ of the two natures.

It was this unique and decisive act of the Holy Spirit in the Incarnation of the eternal Son of God that made possible the virgin birth.

A denial of the plain statements of Matthew and Luke regarding the supernatural conception of Jesus shuts us up to terrible alternatives.

No intelligent, honest-minded person can read the detailed accounts in Matthew 1:18–25 and Luke 1: 26–35 without feeling that both writers were convinced in their own minds that Christ was miraculously born of Mary by the operation of the Holy Spirit.

Are the critics prepared to refute the authority of Matthew, one of the twelve apostles, whose Gospel must have been written when many of the near relations of Joseph and Mary were still alive? Surely

34

those close to the holy family would have denounced Matthew's story if it had been false! As for Luke, the beloved physician, we know that he wrote for the express purpose of setting in order authentic facts which were "most surely believed" by the early church. Luke himself claimed to have had "perfect understanding of all things from the very first," because of his close acquaintance with "eyewitnesses, and ministers of the word." He wanted Theophilus to "know the certainty of those things" wherein he had been instructed (Luke 1:1–4).

If, in their blindness and hardness of heart, men are prepared to deny such overwhelming evidence, they must believe: (1) That Christ was born of natural generation. (2) That He might even have been an illegitimate child of Mary. (3) That He, like all other men, inherited original sin from Adam. In that case He was not sinless.

That Joseph was not the father of Jesus is clear, not only from the distinct statement in Matthew 1:18–20, but also from the recorded pedigree of Joseph himself. In his ancestral line is the name of Jeconias or Jeconiah (the altered form of Jehoiachin) who was the son of Jehoiakim king of Judah (Matt. 1:11; Jer. 22:24). Of this king it was prophesied that "Never shall a son of his attain to sit on David's throne" (Jer. 22:30, Moffatt's translation).

Thus Jeconiah and his seed—which included Joseph—were forever disinherited from the kingdom of Israel. Had Jesus been the real son of Joseph, He could never take the throne of His father David as declared by the angel Gabriel to Mary. How definite was that announcement concerning the Lord Jesus: "The Lord God shall give unto him the throne of his father David; And he shall reign over the house of Jacob forever" (Luke 1:32, 33).

If our blessed Lord had the sinful tendencies inherent in the human race, then He would not be qualified for the unique work of redeeming mankind. "No sinful man purified by the Holy Spirit could have been such a Mediator, for the purification itself is entirely dependent on the propitiation which has been made for sin." [2]

Adam's fall in the Garden of Eden entailed a twofold loss. God lost a son (Adam was a created son of God: Luke 3:38), and that son lost his spiritual life. So Someone was needed who could restore that tragic twofold loss, who could give back to the Father what He had lost and who could restore to Adam what he had forfeited. In other words, a Redeemer must be found.

According to Old Testament law, a redeemer had to be the nearest kinsman. This is beautifully illustrated in the case of Boaz in the Book of Ruth.

Within the limitations of human thought and speech, it can be said with all reverence that Jesus Christ was always God's nearest relation. From eternity He was His only begotten Son. But in order for Christ to become man's "nearest relation" the miracle of the Incarnation was necessary. He must become bone of our bone and flesh of our flesh, and still retain His deity. Such a unique Redeemer, the spotless God-Man, Christ Jesus, came forth into this world through the marvellous operation of the Holy Spirit upon the virgin Mary. In response to utter self-abnegation and trust in God: "Behold the handmaid of the Lord; be it unto me according to thy word," the lowly maid of Nazareth was "overshadowed" by the Holy Ghost, and the Wonder Child of the ages was born.

What a blow to the pride of ancient Greek philosophy was the Holy Spirit's work in the Incarnation! It exposed the false teaching of the Stoics and the

Epicureans who believed that the Deity was detached and unfeeling in His relationship with mankind. The Incarnation brought God so near to the human race that He could not come any nearer. In the words of St. John: "In this was manifested the love of God toward us, because that God sent his only begotten Son into the world." Indeed, now was

> God contracted to a span,
> Incomprehensibly made man.

Only through the Incarnation could Jesus fully qualify to be our Redeemer. By that stupendous miracle of love He earned the right to purchase us back to the Father. The cost was His own blood upon the Cross. For Acts 20:28 tells us plainly that the Church has been purchased with the blood of God.

Such sacred agony upon a felon's gibbet was possible only through the Incarnation. It is no wonder, then, that the saints have always protested against the idea that the Incarnation was mainly exemplary. With adoring wonder they believe it to be primarily redemptive.

Satan hates the glorious truth of the miraculous birth of Jesus through the operation of the Holy Spirit. Thus he blinds even many so-called Bible scholars to the peril they hazard in denying the virgin birth. They come very near to blasphemy against the Holy Ghost!

But the Incarnation was only the beginning of the Holy Spirit's work in relation to Christ's earthly life. When the Master was thirty years of age, He was baptized with the Holy Spirit and thus equipped for His public ministry. His unique, sinless, spotless humanity was not enough for the great work ahead of Him.

To perform those miracles which astonished and

challenged the whole of Jewry, He must needs go to
the Jordan, there to receive the special anointing of
the Holy Spirit. In the words of Acts 10:38: "God
anointed Jesus of Nazareth with the Holy Ghost and
with power: who went about doing good, and healing
all who were oppressed of the devil." That the Incarnate Son of God should need to be filled with the Holy
Spirit is a great mystery; but it has unmistakable sig-
nificance for all Christians today.

To say that "purity is power" is not the whole
truth. Certainly the baptism of the Holy Ghost on
the Day of Pentecost purified the hearts of the hundred
and twenty. Acts 15:8, 9 makes that clear. But the
purification was the prerequisite to the filling of their
hearts with irrepressible love, joy, and power.

Jesus did not need a *purifying* baptism: He was
free from sin. His was the anointing that endued Him
with power for a unique ministry.

It is a striking fact, however, that the Holy Spirit
did not send Jesus into His public ministry immediately after the Jordan baptism. Instead, the Spirit led
Him into the wilderness to be "tempted of the devil."
In Mark's version the language is more vehement, for
there we read that "the Spirit *driveth* him into the
wilderness." [3]

It may well be that Jesus, foreknowing the nature
of the wilderness conflict with Satan, would, in His
human spirit, shrink from that awful ordeal, just as
He afterwards recoiled from the unutterable anguish
of Gethsemane. And so the Holy Spirit, with resist-
less impulse, pressed the anointed Jesus forward into
the arena of combat with Satan in the wilderness.

The same Holy Spirit also instructed Christ in the
tactics needed for such a confrontation. They were
those of prayer and fasting.

Such an extraordinary experience in the wilderness

had more than one result. It not only prepared Jesus to meet the blandishments of Satan; it also enabled Him to fully explore the glorious potential of a life filled with the Holy Ghost. Thus, when the wilderness temptations had ended, "Jesus returned in the power of the Spirit into Galilee: and there went out a fame of him through all the region round about." [4]

We do not read of a single miracle being performed by the sinless Jesus *before* His Jordan baptism. But, on emerging in triumph from the wilderness, He went forth to be more than conqueror in every realm into which He entered. Disease vanished at His touch; demons fled before His command; and even the dead came back to life at His decree.

It cannot be over-emphasized that all these miracles were wrought by Jesus in the power of the Holy Spirit who so fully possessed Him. That is why He could make those two striking statements: "I cast out demons by the Spirit of God" (Matt. 12:28); and "He that believeth on me, the works that I do shall he do also; and greater works than these shall he do; because I go unto my Father" (John 14:12).

Jesus knew full well that the Holy Spirit, who filled His own being throughout His earthly ministry, would operate in the same miraculous way when Pentecost had come to His disciples. And so it came to pass.

It was also through the inspiration of the Holy Spirit that Christ gave forth His unrivaled teaching on the Kingdom of God. We are told that "he through the Holy Ghost" gave "commandments unto the apostles whom he had chosen" (Acts 1:2). The Father, through the Holy Spirit, gave His beloved Son those words to speak which astonished the people: "for he taught them as one that had authority, and not as the scribes" (Mark 1:22).

Jesus, with prophetic insight, promised His obedient followers that "the Holy Ghost shall teach you
in that same hour what ye ought to say" (Luke 12:12).
He knew that the same Holy Ghost, who had anointed
Him for His teaching ministry, would also give heavenly wisdom and utterance to sanctified Christians,
according to their need.

Right to the end of the journey on earth, the blessed Holy Spirit gave Jesus all He needed to finish the
work His Father had given Him to do. In that supreme
moment, when Christ "offered himself without spot
to God" as an atonement for sin, it was "through the
eternal Spirit" that He was enabled to do it (Heb.
9:14).

Even when the journey was over and the Saviour's
dead body was in the tomb—His soul had entered
Hades—the Holy Spirit's special relationship with the
human Jesus had not ended. For it was through the
miraculous operation of the Holy Ghost that Jesus was
raised from the dead. Romans 8:11 leaves us in no
doubt on that important issue. It reads: "For if the
Spirit of him that raised up Jesus from the dead dwell
in you, he that raised up Christ from the dead shall
also quicken your mortal bodies by his Spirit that
dwelleth in you."

> 'Twas by the Holy Spirit's might
> That resurrection's work was done—
> The Paraclete's attested right
> To glorify God's matchless Son.

---

1 Galatians 4:6; Romans 8:9
2 Howard Watkin-Jones in *The Holy Spirit from Arminius to
  Wesley*, p. 200
3 Mark 1:12
4 Luke 4:14

CHAPTER FIVE

The Holy Spirit in Human Experience

IT IS NOT ENOUGH to have an intellectual conception of the deity and operations of the Holy Spirit. Only a vital personal experience of His indwelling will fully satisfy the human heart.

A remarkable story is told concerning Dr. Walter Wilson, the well-known American Methodist preacher-physician. After his conversion to Christ he became a lover of the Bible and sought to serve the Lord in teaching, preaching and tract distribution. But his manifold activities seemed to produce little result. This ineffectiveness troubled him, but he was exhorted by Christian friends "not to look for results, but only to be busy at seed sowing."

Then came an unforgettable crisis in his life. A missionary from France visited Dr. Wilson's home and asked him the searching question: "What is the Holy Spirit to you?"

Wilson gave the orthodox answer: "He is one of the persons of the Godhead—a Teacher, a Guide, the Third Person of the Trinity."

The missionary then rebuked the doctor by pointing out that he had not given the Holy Spirit His rightful place. He said: "He is just as great, just as precious, just as needful as the other two persons of the Trinity. But still you have not answered my question: What is He to you?"

The crestfallen Wilson was obliged to give the truthful answer: "He is nothing to me. I have no contact with Him, no powerful relationship, and could get along quite well without Him."

Back came the reply which caused the doctor to inwardly tremble: "It is because of this that your life is so fruitless even though your efforts are so great. If you will seek personally to know the Holy Spirit He will transform your life."

Dr. Walter Wilson never rested until he obtained a personal Pentecost and realized the glorious indwelling of the Holy Spirit. It was this personal experience of the Holy Ghost that revolutionized his Christian life and service and made him a marvelous soul winner and Bible teacher.

It is imperative that mental conception of the Holy Spirit should not outweigh inward experience. The two should go hand-in-hand, for God never meant them to be mutually exclusive. We are to "grow in grace and in knowledge." If the modern Pentecostal Movement is lacking in eminent theologians, it is also true that in many so-called evangelical circles there is a scarcity of white-hot witnesses to the Spirit-filled experience.

Paul was concerned that the Corinthian Christians should not be ignorant about spiritual gifts; therefore he gave them sound teaching on that important but controversial theme. As W. P. Paterson has put it: "It would be a serious blemish on the perfect religion if, in making provision for our spiritual needs, it left us in a condition of intellectual oppression and dissatisfaction."—*The Rule of Faith*, p. 215.

It is a fact, however, that with the growth of intellectual attainment in the study of the Holy Spirit down the centuries, there came a gradual departure from that intense love of Scripture quotation which characterized the post-apostolic divines. Philosophy and logic received increasing attention as a basis for establishing doctrine. It has been pointed out that by the 14th and 15th centuries the current style of theological writing was practically sermonic, institutional and confessional.

The coming of the great 16th-century Reformation brought men back to the Bible as the firm ground of their beliefs. Thus we find in the writings of men like Luther and Calvin that their "pneumatology" was based on their belief in the absolute authority of Scripture, inspired by the Holy Spirit, as the rule of faith.

When, in the early part of the 18th century, England was steeped in infidelity and immorality, it was not Bishop Joseph Butler's famous *Analogy of Religion* that saved the day. His scholarly arguments, while they dealt massive blows upon the Deistic speculation so prevalent at that time, left the masses utterly godless and indifferent.

It was John Wesley's experimental religion that shook England with an amazing evangelical revival. Good Bishop Butler's polemics did not save his country from the bloody revolution that threatened her. What did it was the emphasis of Wesley and his co-workers on the doctrine of the Holy Spirit, with its assurance of present salvation (i.e., the knowledge of sins forgiven, the new birth, and entire sanctification), and a host of witnesses whose completely transformed lives gave undeniable evidence of the validity of such a doctrine.

It is pathetic that while Butler earnestly desired a moral transformation in England, he strongly deprecated anything that savored of religious enthusiasm. He once said to John Wesley: "Sir, the pretending to extraordinary revelations and gifts of the Holy Ghost is a horrid thing, a very horrid thing."

The wise and practical Wesley replied: "I pretend to no extraordinary revelations or gifts of the Holy Ghost: none but what every Christian may receive, and ought to expect and pray for."

But when the learned Bishop came to die, he could not rest until he had received the very assurance of present salvation he had deemed impossible of knowing.

Summoning his chaplain, he said to him: "Though I have endeavored to avoid sin, and to please God to the utmost of my power, yet, from the consciousness of perpetual infirmities, I am still afraid to die."

His chaplain replied: "My lord, you have forgotten that Jesus Christ is a Saviour."

"True," said the Bishop, "but how shall I know that He is a Saviour for me?"

"My lord," answered the chaplain, "it is written, 'Him that cometh to me I will in no wise cast out.' "

"True," said the dying Bishop Butler, "and I am surprised that, although I have read that Scripture a thousand times over, I have never felt its virtue till this moment; and now I die happy."

In view of the present rapidly increasing tendency to link up with the Church of Rome, we need to repeatedly ask the question: Will the papacy alter any of its fundamental doctrines as laid down in the famous Council of Trent? Let us never forget that the Council of Trent pronounced definitely *against* any direct witness of the Holy Spirit to the spirit of the individual believer, assuring him of his present salvation and acceptance with God.

We badly need a revival in the preaching of the doctrine of the witness of the Holy Spirit. For no man can be truly happy unless he has assurance about the vital things of life. Scripture makes it plain that divine certification of present, full salvation is given to obedient men and women through the operation of the Holy Ghost. Hallelujah! How precious are such words as these:

"The Spirit himself beareth witness with our spirit, that we *are* the children of God" (Rom. 8:16). "For by one offering he hath perfected for ever them that are sanctified. Whereof also the Holy Ghost is a witness to us" (Heb. 10:14, 15).

We should never rest satisfied until we have the clear witness of the Holy Spirit to our regeneration and entire sanctification.

CHAPTER SIX

The Sanctifying Spirit

Dr. A. B. Simpson used to tell the story of a woman in Chicago who came forward with eagerness to the altar at a meeting where he presided. She said to Dr. Simpson, "I am seeking the blessing of sanctification."

He replied: "Is it the person of the Holy Ghost you want?"

"No," she said, "the blessing of sanctification."

The saintly and experienced Dr. Simpson then answered: "Your sanctification is not a blessing. It is a person—the blessed Holy Ghost. He is made unto you wisdom, righteousness, sanctification. When you receive the Holy Ghost, He brings Christ and makes Him your sanctification. You put your faith in God the Father?"

"Yes," she replied.

"Have you faith in God the Son?"

"Yes."

"Have you ever put faith in God the Holy Ghost?"

"No," she answered.

Said Dr. Simpson: "That is what you want then. Receive the Holy Ghost and you will have no trouble about sanctification."

Of course, Dr. Simpson's statements need clarification. In my own personal dealing with Christians at the altar of prayer I have found those who were truly "born again" of the Holy Spirit, but who confessed their great need of entire sanctification. Doubtless what Dr. Simpson meant was that the Holy Spirit is the only One who can lead God's people into the glorious experience of a heart made pure and filled with perfect love. And He does that when He himself fully possesses the consecrated, trusting Christian.

It is one thing to be born again of the Holy Spirit. It is another thing to be *filled* with the Spirit.

The tragedy of the Corinthian Christians to whom Paul wrote was this: Although they exercised wonderful gifts of the Holy Spirit, such as prophecy and tongues, yet they were still carnal in heart. There is only one true explanation of this mystery: it is that the Corinthian Christians were not filled with the Holy Ghost at the time of Paul's indictment—"ye are yet carnal" (I Cor. 3:3). For no person who is fully possessed by the Holy Spirit can, at the same time, be carnal or unsanctified. As well might a room be said to be filled with light when patches of darkness remain. To contend for such a contradiction is a libel upon the Holy Ghost himself.

John Wesley proclaimed a doctrine of Scriptural holiness in which the work of the Holy Spirit was given the utmost emphasis. In his sermon on "The Scripture Way of Salvation" he says: "We feel 'the love of God shed abroad in our heart by the Holy Ghost which is given unto us,' producing love to all mankind, and more especially to the children of God; expelling the love of the world, the love of pleasure, of ease, of honor, of money; together with pride, anger, self-will, and every other evil temper—in a word, changing the earthly, sensual, devilish mind into 'the mind which was in Christ Jesus.'"

In his sermon on "The Holy Ghost" Wesley gives rightful honor to the Paraclete. He declares: "The title Holy, applied to the Spirit of God, does not only denote that He is holy in His own nature, but that He makes us so."

Lancelot Andrewes delighted in referring to the Comforter as "the sanctifying Spirit." And how right he was in his discernment of this operation of the Holy Ghost in the human heart. As John Owen reminds us, "the sanctification which the Spirit works within man after conversion affects the whole spirit, soul, and body." [1]

In the recent manifestations of the Holy Spirit among Christians of old-time denominations in the U.S.A., much has been said about the miraculous gifts of the Comforter which are in operation. We rejoice in this divine quickening among Episcopalians, Lutherans, Methodists, Baptists, and other sections of the Christian Church. But a note of charitable warning should be sounded lest undue emphasis on the "glossolalia" obscures the greater work of the Holy Ghost in the renovation of our nature into the image of Jesus Christ.

When the Holy Ghost came at Pentecost to fill the hearts of the hundred-and-twenty, the visible symbol was not a dove. It was a cloven tongue like fire—the emblem of dynamic purification. Jesus had no need of purification from inbred sin: He had no taint of depravity. Hence the symbol of the Holy Spirit who came "without measure" to the spotless Son of God was a dove.

But fallen man must be purified from inward depravity in order to enter into heaven. For "without the sanctification no man shall see the Lord" (Heb. 12:14, RV).

The major question in theology is this: Can a hu-

man being be cleansed from all sin in this life? If he
cannot. then when and where does this purification
take place? Surely not at death, for death is an enemy
and not a deliverer from sin. The seat of sin is in
the soul, not in the body. It is "the soul that sinneth":
the body is but the vehicle of the soul.

Unless we believe in a sort of purgatory in the
after-life (which God forbid!), then we are compelled
to admit that at some time this side of death, the soul
of man can be made pure. This is gloriously possible
because of the perfect work of Christ at Calvary. For
on the Cross Jesus not only bare our sins that penitent
sinners might be freely pardoned; on the tree He also
took our "old man" that the "body of sin might be
destroyed" (Rom. 6:6). By the "old man" is meant our
old, natural selves before we were saved by the grace
of God. The "body of sin" refers to that indwelling
corruption with which we were born. It cannot mean
the human body as such; for our bodies are to be "the
temples of the Holy Ghost." We are to glorify God in
our body, which belongs to Him (I Cor. 6:19, 20).

It is the special work of the Holy Ghost, as Executive of the Godhead, to make real *in us* what the Lord
Jesus did *for us* on the cross. The noted Scottish divine, John Cameron (1579–1625) contended that it
was only through the sanctifying Spirit of God that
a vital union with Christ is possible. Through the Holy
Ghost we appropriate the merits of Christ's atonement,
thereby securing our full deliverance from sin.

Many good Christians insist upon a particular outward manifestation as being the infallible evidence of
a Spirit-baptized life. The deep inward work of perfect
cleansing from sin and the filling of the whole being
with the love of God is sometimes overlooked in the
heat of contention for a certain point of view. Yet those
same good people will sing earnestly hymns which

specially emphasize the sanctifying operations of the Holy Ghost. Here are extracts from some of them:

> Loving Spirit, make me loving,
> Melt my heart and cleanse from sin,
> Satisfy my restless longings,
> Make me fair and pure within.
>
> —Annie M. Potter

> O Unction from on high,
> Come, permeate within;
> Then I shall bear Thy searching eye
> Without a trace of sin.
>
> —D. P. Williams

> Lord, as of old at Pentecost
> Thou didst Thy power display
> With cleansing, purifying flame
> Descend on us today.
> All self consume, all sin destroy!
> With earnest zeal endue
> Each waiting heart to work for Thee;
> Oh Lord, our faith renew!
>
> —Charlotte G. Homer

> To make an end of sin,
> And Satan's works destroy,
> He brings His kingdom in,
> Peace, righteousness, and joy;
> The Holy Ghost to man is given;
> Rejoice in God sent down from heaven.
>
> —Charles Wesley

Often, when singing from our hearts the songs of Zion, we forget our set doctrinal views and give expression to our inward longings. Alone with God, shut up in His holy presence, the real Christian yearns above all else to be like Jesus. Instinctively he appeals to the Third Person of the Trinity and cries:

O Thou Spirit Divine,
All my nature refine,
Till the beauty of Jesus be seen in me.

When God inspires any of His saints to compose a hymn, it is for the benefit of the *whole* Church—and not for any particular denomination.

No sect dares to monopolize such hymns as: "When I Survey the Wondrous Cross," and "Rock of Ages, Cleft for Me." They are the property of all the saints, for they express eternal truths.

So it is with God-inspired hymns on the Holy Spirit. Despite our cut-and-dried theology on the Holy Spirit, we sense the truth of His sanctifying grace when singing from our hearts.

Some years ago I talked with the late Principal Percy Parker, a saintly Pentecostal leader in Britain. One thing he said on that occasion has lived with me. It was this: "We have had gifts and prophecy. Our need is sanctification."

If, at all times, we will honor the Holy Spirit by seeking the more excellent way of perfect love, He will see to it that we are equipped with those gifts which are so valuable in Christian service.

---

[1] *Concerning the Holy Spirit*, p. 255

CHAPTER SEVEN

The Spirit Marches On

ONE OF THE GREATEST MIRACLES in history was the impact of the early Christian Church upon the pagan Roman Empire. Just think of what really happened.

On the Day of Pentecost in A.D. 33, a mere 120 people—mostly working class folk—left an upper room in Jerusalem to spread a certain message to the uttermost part of earth. What was that message? Simply this: that a Jew named Jesus of Nazareth, who was crucified under Pontius Pilate, had risen from the dead and was alive for evermore. Further, that He was the Messiah, and that through His name alone was salvation given to all who would repent and believe.

From a human standpoint the task of that small group was hopeless. Apart from the hundred-and-twenty, only a limited number of other disciples claimed to have seen this Jesus since He was supposed to have risen from the dead. And was not He a Jew, a member of a hated and despised race? To make things worse, had not His own countrymen rejected and crucified Him? And worse still, did not the mighty Roman empire fiercely persecute this "sect of the Nazarene"? How, then, could they succeed in their gigantic task?

In his book *The Trial of Jesus*, Walter M. Chandler has stated: "No period of human history is so marked by lust and licentiousness as the history of Rome at the beginning of the Christian era. The destruction of infants and the gladiatorial games were mere epitomes of Roman brutality and degeneracy. Barbarity, corruption, and dissoluteness pervaded every form of Roman life."

Professor H. B. Workman has reminded us that for 200 years the mere profession of Christianity itself was a crime. "Christianus sum" (I am a Christian) was almost the one plea for which there was no forgiveness. He who made it was allowed neither to present apology nor call in the aid of a pleader. In those days the Romans, Greeks or Gentiles were known as "the first race." The Jews, admittedly different, were known as "the second race." But the Christians, standing in such marked contrast by their daring unworldliness and uncompromising piety, were stigmatized "the third race." They were "dead to all the globe" and out of joint with the world's policies and expediences. There rang out the cry in the circus of Carthage: "How long must we endure this third race?"

One poet has expressed it thus:

> "So to the wild wolf hate
> Were sacrificed
> The panting, huddling flock
> Whose crime was Christ."

It was in such an atmosphere and against such terrible odds that the early Christians lived, suffered and died. But what a glorious triumph was theirs!

At the close of the first century A.D., Justin Martyr, the well-known Christian apologist, could truly testify: "There is not a nation, either Greek or Barbarian, or of any other name, even those who wander in tribes or live in tents, among whom prayers and thanksgivings are not offered to the Father and Creator of the universe in the name of the crucified Jesus."

What was the secret of such amazing success? It was not in superb organization or human genius. It was in the operation of the Holy Spirit through sancti-fied, obedient men and women. The recurring note in the Acts of the Apostles is the fulness of the Holy Spirit in human lives. Again and again we read of humble Christians who were "filled with the Holy Ghost."

At least four characteristics marked those Spirit-filled disciples mentioned in Acts, chapters 4 and 5. They were: *Great power*: "With great power gave the apostles witness of the Lord Jesus" (4:33). *Great grace*: "And great grace was upon them all" (4:33). *Great fear*: "And great fear came upon all the church" (5: 11). *Great increase*: "And the believers were the more added to the Lord, multitudes both of men and women" (5:4).

Christ promised His disciples that they would re-ceive power when the Holy Ghost had come upon them (Acts 1:8). On the day of Pentecost that prom-ise was fulfilled. It was a power that gave boldness to witness for Christ, and which lifted the early Christians into the realm of the miraculous.

"They spake the word with boldness" is the ringing note in Acts 4:31. No longer was Peter a cringing coward before a little maid. Now he boldly faced the enemies of Jesus and told them they were the mur-derers of the Messiah. It was the *boldness* of Peter and John that caused the Sanhedrin to marvel and to acknowledge "that they had been with Jesus" (Acts 4:13).

Holy boldness in witnessing for Christ always marks Spirit-filled believers.

Everywhere with shoutings loud,
Shouts that shake the gates of hell,
Thy anointed witness cloud
Of Thy great redemption tell.

Some years ago, when preaching in the State of Oregon, U.S.A., I had a surprise. A prominent member of the local holiness church confessed her need of entire sanctification. A splendid worker in the assembly and the daughter of a fine minister, she seemed to have no need of the baptism of the Spirit. But in the searching light of divine truth she humbled herself and cried out for *full* salvation. God met her need and filled her with the Holy Spirit. Giving her testimony afterwards, she said that in spite of her mental conception of sanctification she had not the power to witness for Christ to a certain neighbor. She knew her duty, but failed to do it. Now, with radiant face, she told of glorious victory. Almost the first thing she did after the Holy Ghost had come in sanctifying fulness was to witness to that same neighbor. The Comforter had given her boldness to glorify Christ in testimony.

But Pentecost also lifts the Christian into the realm of the supernatural. The early disciples proved this to be true. Had not Jesus plainly stated that if they truly believed on Him, then the works that He did on earth would be repeated in their ministry? (John 14: 12). Filled with the Holy Spirit, they entered into their inheritance—the ministry of the miraculous.

Not only "by the hands of the apostles were many signs and wonders wrought among the people" (Acts 5:12); the more lowly placed members of the church also shared in the exploits of the Spirit in the realm of divine healing. Both Stephen and Philip, who gladly "served tables" in the daily ministration, "did great wonders and miracles among the people."

And so the ministry of the miraculous continued to the final chapter of the Acts. Yes, and right down the centuries wherever the Holy Spirit was honored and obeyed by Christian believers.

Gibbon, the noted historian, has admitted in his *Decline and Fall of the Roman Empire* that one reason for the astonishing advance of the early church was its claim to miraculous powers.

If we say we are filled with the Holy Spirit, then the non-Christian has a right to demand tangible proof of this in the character and ministry of the followers of Jesus. Certainly we should "covet earnestly the best gifts" of the Holy Spirit. They are weapons in the divine armory with which God equips His loyal soldiers.

A word of caution is needed here, however, lest fanaticism creep in.

Many people are willing to pray for hours to be filled with "great power." They long for the gifts of miracles, prophecy, healing and tongues, et cetera. But how many Christians yearn to be filled with "great grace"—to be like Jesus in meekness, love, and long-suffering? Heated arguments about the more spectacular manifestations of the Spirit (including the glossolalia) have often engaged the minds of God's children. But I have never yet listened to an animated discussion on the necessity of "helps"—that valuable but despised gift of the Holy Ghost (I Cor. 12:28)!

Writing to a Miss Bolton on December 5, 1772, John Wesley cautioned: "George Bell, William Green, and many others, then full of love, were favoured with extraordinary revelations and manifestations from God. But by this very thing Satan beguiled them from the simplicity that is in Christ. By insensible degrees they were led to value these extraordinary gifts more than the ordinary grace of God; and I could not convince them that a grain of humble love was better than all these gifts put together. This, my dear friend, was what made me fear for you."

"Great grace" is always the concomitant of "great power" in the truly Spirit-filled life. Our Lord Jesus was full of grace and truth. And the apostle John could testify: "And of his fulness have all we received, and grace for grace" (John 1:16). The Pentecostal believers of Acts 4:33 possessed not only "great power"; they were also endued with "great grace."

This abundant grace manifested itself in at least three ways, viz., in perfect unity, in practical charity, in pervading serenity. We read that they were "of one heart and one soul" (Acts 4:32). Although of diverse personality and temperament, they were enabled by the Holy Ghost to adjust themselves to one another. The baptism of the Holy Ghost did not steam-roller over their varied personalities nor did it destroy their purely natural appetites and instincts. But it gave them the fruit of love, meekness, and self-control (temperance) (Gal. 5:22, 23). Entirely sanctified Christians are always "endeavouring to keep the unity of the Spirit in the bond of peace."

Satan's master stroke is to destroy the bond of holy love between the saints. I once heard a missionary from Malaya say that the biggest single problem on many mission fields in the Far East was the lack of unity among the leaders themselves!

Satan did his utmost to disrupt the unity of the apostolic church. Into the communal life of those early Christians crept a nationalistic spirit. There "arose a murmuring of the Grecians against the Hebrews, because their widows were neglected in the daily ministration" (Acts 6:1). Quick to detect this subtle move of the devil, the apostles nipped it in the bud through the appointment of seven Spirit-filled deacons to "serve tables."

Even in the most spiritual churches differences of opinion will often arise. But they are quickly resolved when the Holy Spirit is allowed His presidential rights. And His method is to bestow "great grace upon them all."

When it comes to practical charity as an evidence of "great grace," then the early church sets a perfect example. Of them we read that "they had all things common" (Acts 4:32). Those Spirit-filled Christians were considerate and compassionate one for the other. They distributed to the necessities of their less fortunate brethren and sisters. Like Job of old, they "sought out" the cause of the needy.

Paul declared that the "love of God is shed abroad in our hearts by the Holy Ghost" (Rom. 5:5). But it was John who applied a searching test of that love when he wrote: "Whoso hath this world's goods, and seeth his brother have need, and shutteth up his bowels of compassion from him, how dwelleth the love of God in him?" (I John 3:17).

John Wesley believed in a holiness that was social and ethical. In 1776 he received notice from the Commissioners of Excise, stating "they cannot doubt but you have plate for which you have hitherto neglected to make an entry." Wesley's reply was characteristic of the man. It was: "I have two silver spoons at London and two at Bristol. This is all the plate I have at present, and I shall not buy any more while so many round me want bread."

Another mark of "great grace" in the early Christians was what could be called "pervading serenity." Tertullian talked about the "hilarity of the saints." And how right he was. Not that he meant the empty cackle and frivolity that sometimes masquerades as the joy of the Lord. Doubtless he referred to that holy serenity possessed by Spirit-filled Christians, which defied and pervaded the worst of circumstances.

Not only in the flood-tide of revival did New Testament believers "eat their meat with gladness and singleness of heart, praising God" (Acts 2:46, 47).

Even when the fierce gales of persecution were blowing, and the apostles were wrongfully imprisoned and beaten, "they departed from the council, rejoicing that they were counted worthy to suffer shame for his name" (Acts 5:41).

The fruit of the Spirit is joy.

It is when we come to the expression "great fear"—as a mark of deep spirituality—that some people are puzzled. Yet there is the plain statement in Acts 5:11 that "great fear came upon all the church."

What does it mean? Surely not the carnal terror which seizes the wicked when the judgments of God are falling upon them. In reference to the Spirit-baptized Christians of Acts 5 it means something quite different. For the Greek word *phobos*, translated "fear," can be defined only according to its context.

A few examples from the New Testament prove this:

Matthew 28:8—"And they departed quickly from the sepulchre with fear and great joy."

Acts 9:31—"The churches throughout all Judea and Galilee and Samaria . . . walking in the fear of the Lord and the comfort of the Holy Ghost, were multiplied."

Ephesians 5:21—"Submitting yourselves one to another in the fear of God."

Thus we see that the fear begotten of a Spirit-filled experience goes hand-in-hand with holy joy, comfort and meekness. In fact this kind of fear is simply a deep reverence and awe; a profound wonder and ap-

preciation of the grace and mercy of God towards
penitent sinners.

We live in an age of irreverence when, in the name
of liberty and democracy, license and callousness
abound. The atmosphere of jazz and rock-and-roll
permeates almost every sphere of life. Even the precious songs of Zion are sometimes "swung" and not
"sung." The sacred things of eternity are parodied by
creatures who live only for time and sense.

It is tragic that something of this lack of reverence
has crept into evangelical churches. Again and again,
in my travels, I have been pained at heart by the
conduct of professing saints in the sanctuary. They
have so taken things for granted; they have become so
used to their privileges, that they are flippant and
talkative even when the preacher is praying aloud or
declaring the oracles of God. Of course, if the platform
sets a bad example, we cannot wholly blame the pew
for doing likewise!

It is high time we got back to the atmosphere of
sanctified worship. It is true that outward posture is
not an infallible sign of holy reverence. Nevertheless,
the act of kneeling, both in private and public prayer,
is to be commended. The example of our Lord himself,
along with that of Paul and Daniel, should encourage
us to kneel in prayer. Read Luke 22:41; Acts 20:36;
and Daniel 6:10 in this connection.

William Penn said of the illustrious George Fox,
founder of the Quakers: "The most reverent frame I
ever beheld was his in prayer."

No wonder the "man with the leathern breeches"
shook England in the 17th century!

The inevitable outcome of "great" power, grace,
and fear, through the indwelling Holy Spirit is great
increase. Fertility is always in God's plan for His
obedient children. Barrenness is a reproach to the

cause of Him who declared: "I will build my church, and the gates of hell shall not prevail against it." Thus it should come as no surprise to read in Acts 5:14 that "believers were the more added to the Lord, multitudes both of men and women."

The Holy Spirit is pledged to glorify the risen Christ. He can never be a failure in promoting the Kingdom of God on earth. But He patiently waits for the co-operation of sanctified saints. He marches on through those who have fully yielded to Him and who expect His omnipotent power to vanquish the hosts of darkness. For "when the enemy comes in like a flood," it is "the Spirit of the Lord" who puts him to flight (Isa. 59:19).

The Holy Spirit was in Jerusalem when Christ was crucified. In fact He was *with* the apostles before the day of Pentecost (John 14:17). But it was only when the Holy Spirit *filled* the hearts of the hundred-and-twenty that deep conviction seized the Jews in Jerusalem, and three thousand sinners were saved in one day. The mighty revival broke out in the hardest city in the world because the Holy Spirit was in full control of the Church of Jesus.

It is a fact of history that within 30 years of the day of Pentecost, the gospel of Christ had spread from Palestine to Syria, through the numerous districts of Asia Minor and the islands of the Aegean Sea, into Greece and North Africa, and even into Rome itself.

The gospel age began with revival and ruin: revival in A.D. 33 in Jerusalem, and ruin upon the Jewish nation not many years afterwards.

The gospel age will close with revival and ruin. Iniquity will abound, sinners will wax worse and worse. But a Spirit-baptized Church will increase mightily in holiness and power on the eve of Christ's return.

Said the Holy Spirit through the prophet Daniel

concerning "the time of the end": "Many shall be purified, and made white, and tried; but the wicked shall do wickedly" (Dan. 12:10).

Let us honor and obey the Holy Spirit in these closing days of the dispensation. Then we shall see Him marching on.

CHAPTER EIGHT

Rivers of Living Water

IT WAS AT A CONVENTION in Cornwall. After preaching on the text John 7:38, 39, I went into the counselling room where an intelligent youth was seeking earnestly to be filled with the Holy Spirit. Almost tearfully he told me that about twelve months previously he had asked the Lord for the Holy Spirit. "But," he said, "I have only a trickle." He longed for the "rivers of living water" that Jesus had promised to those who believe on Him. He belonged to that host of Christians who say to the Lord:

> "Rivers" is Thy promise,
> This shall be our plea,
> Less than this can never
> Meet our cry for Thee:
> Tired of lukewarm service,
> And the loss it brings,
> We would live entirely
> For eternal things.

Most of Christ's important statements about the Holy Spirit are found in John's Gospel. None is more vivid than His promise in chapter 7, verses 38 and 39: "He that believeth in me, as the scripture hath said, from within him [his innermost being] shall flow rivers

of living water. But this spake he of the Spirit, which
they that believed on him were to receive."

It was on the final day of the Feast of Tabernacles
that Jesus uttered such stirring words. This festival
lasted for seven days, although an eighth day was
added as a time of "holy convocation."

Every morning, for seven days, a procession headed
by a priest and accompanied with music went from
the Temple of Jerusalem to the Pool of Siloam. There
the priest filled a golden vase with water and carried
it to the Temple amid the joyful shouts of the people.
Then he poured the water upon the western side of
the altar of burnt offerings. At the same time another
priest poured a drink offering of wine upon the eastern
side of the altar. During this act the congregation
chanted the words of the "Hallel" (Psalms 113 to 119).

This symbolism was undoubtedly connected with
the gift of the latter rain, which was at that season. It
spoke also of the gift of water which was so vital in
the East. The Jews at the Feast of Tabernacles must
have recalled that time when, as their fathers thirsted
in the wilderness, the life-giving waters gushed from
the rock smitten by Moses.

It was on the last great day of the feast, probably
the eighth, that Jesus stood up and made His dramatic
announcement. It was all the more dramatic because
(as some Bible scholars believe) no water was carried
from the Pool of Siloam on the eighth day. It was the
waterless day.

In His revolutionary statement Jesus spoke of the
promise, purpose, and pathway of the Holy Spirit's
fulness in the human heart.

1. *The promise of the Spirit's fulness*

No promise in the Old Testament is more important
than the coming of the Holy Spirit to indwell and em-

power the soul of man. Ever since Adam, through the Fall in Eden, had lost the grace and indwelling of the Holy Spirit, men had groaned in their bondage and longed for their forfeited inheritance. But in their own strength they were powerless to regain what, in Adam, they had lost. However, the darkened sky had been lightened by God's gracious promise that one day the Holy Spirit would return in plentitude to indwell the sons of men. Through Isaiah, Ezekiel and Joel that promise was reiterated (Isa. 44:3; Ezek. 36:26, 27; Joel 2:28, 29).

When Jesus came He confirmed and clarified what He termed "the promise of the Father." By His atoning death, resurrection and ascension He made possible the fulfillment of that promise. Being exalted to the throne of God, He received of the Father the promise of the Holy Ghost, that He might "pour" Him upon obedient hearts (Acts 2:33).

It is vital to note that Christ's promise of the fulness of the Spirit was not made to sinners. It was for His disciples, for those who believe on Him. Elsewhere (John 14:17) Jesus plainly said that the world could not receive the Comforter. The only persons who are eligible for the baptism of the Holy Ghost are those who have really trusted Jesus to save them.

Writing to the Ephesians Paul declared: "After that ye believed [in Christ], ye were sealed with that Holy Spirit of promise" (Eph. 1:13). His own experience was of like order. Gloriously converted to Christ on the Damascus Road, Paul was filled with the Holy Spirit three days later under the ministry of Ananias (Acts 9:6, 11–17).

The same order of events was witnessed in the revival in Samaria. Philip preached Christ to the Samaritans, and many believed on Jesus and were publicly baptized in His name. The converts exulted in their new-found experience: "and there was a great joy in that city." But it was a little time afterwards that these Samaritan converts were filled with the Holy Ghost (Acts 8:5–8, 12, 15–17).

As a lad of thirteen years I was truly saved. The power of sin was broken in my life and I became a new creature in Christ Jesus. But it was not until some years later that I was filled with the Holy Spirit.

Wherever I go I find Christians who are longing for a life of power and victory. Their great need is to to be filled with the Holy Ghost.

It seems to me such a pity that the thousands of converts in many large evangelistic campaigns of today are not immediately given clear teaching on this vital subject, and urged to seek their personal Pentecost.

2. *The purpose of the Spirit's fulness*

Unless we are clear on this important point we shall go away frustrated and fearful. It is plain from the teaching of Jesus and the apostles that the grand purpose of the fulness of the Holy Ghost is to purify and empower the life of the Christian.

How significant is the emphasis Jesus placed upon the penetration of the Holy Spirit in a believer's heart. "Out of his *innermost being* shall flow rivers of living water."

The Greek word *koilia* (translated "belly" in the A.V.) speaks of the very foundation of human personality, or as the mystics might render it, "the central depths" of the soul. This teaches us that before there can be the *outflow* of divine power from our lives there must be the *incoming* of the Holy Spirit to possess the deepest recesses of our being.

And it must never be forgotten that the Holy Spirit is not some magnetic influence flowing from heaven into human hearts, in order to galvanize them into

Christian activity. The Holy Spirit is a divine person, the Third Person of the Godhead.

Over 90 times in Scripture the adjective "holy" is used of the Spirit. He is the Spirit of holiness; and so it is inconceivable that any indwelling sin can remain in the heart when He has penetrated into and fully possessed the *koilia* of our personality. The Holy Spirit comes to give us, as it were, a spiritual "spring cleaning." He enters not only into the upper stories and ground floor of our being; He possesses also the basement of our personality. The subconscious is cleansed by His all-pervasive efficacy. There are plenty of Christians who long for power and yet are unwilling for the deep inward cleansing of their nature.

I had a big surprise when preaching in a holiness church in California some years ago. A young lady was seeking the Spirit's fulness, and seemed to be in earnest. But when I told her that inner purity preceded the outflow of divine power, she exclaimed: "Cannot I be filled with the Holy Spirit without having a pure heart?" I replied: "No, you cannot." Realizing the true purpose of the Holy Spirit for her life, she refused to obey the light from heaven and left the counseling room sadder than when she had entered it.

How illuminating is Ezekiel's vision of the life-giving, healing waters that flowed from under the altar in the house of God. Those waters are clearly a picture of the Spirit-filled life from which issue the streams of divine grace and power, bringing blessing and healing to needy humanity. But it is significant that the living waters did not begin to flow until the altar had been thoroughly purged and purified (ch. 43:26). So it is with the Christian life. The altar of the heart must be entirely sanctified by the Holy Spirit before the coveted power can flow out. This is always the divine order.

Samuel Chadwick made a revealing confession when he said: "The blessing I sought was power. The blessing God had for me began further in and deeper down. Power was conditioned. The truth that sanctifies begins with a cleansing of heart and motive, a life surrendered to the divine will, and a personality possessed by and filled with the Holy Spirit." [1]

If purity of heart can be termed the negative side of Pentecost, then the positive side of the blessing is surely power for effective service.

The Holy Ghost does not possess us simply that we might have inward rapture. He comes right into the heart so that He might flow out from us to thirsty souls around. The waters in Ezekiel's vision flowed toward the desert. God the Holy Ghost will never enter any sphere which has no outlet. As William Luff has put it:

> God fills the soul that it may pour
> The fulness on another heart:
> Not that the filled with good may store
> The good God giveth to impart.

Jesus illustrated this life of power by the figure of rivers of living water flowing from the inner depths of the sanctified Christian.

In the Holy Spirit is power that is abundant, spontaneous, irresistible and life-giving. Not a well, or a spring, or even a single river—but "rivers." What a picture of abundance is this! Pentecost always speaks of overflowing fulness—enough and to spare.

The feast of Pentecost was during the wheat harvest in Palestine; at the time of the ripening of the summer fruits. God had promised such abundant crops to an obedient Israel that when Pentecost came, the farmers were to leave the corners of their fields, along with the gleanings, for the benefit of the poor.

Thus it is with the truly Spirit-filled Christian. Not only is he satisfied with what God has given him; he also has an abundant overflow for the needs of others. He knows that Christ has given him birth "to brother all the souls of earth."

Not only is this power of the Spirit in abundant supply: it is also spontaneous. The rivers of living water *flow* (they are not forced) from the inner depths of the purified heart. We have to pump water from a well or else let down a bucket to get a supply. But rivers flow spontaneously.

How tragic is the spectacle of Christian leaders trying to *organize* faith, or prayer, or love. It simply cannot be done. It is just like forcing an unwilling horse to the water trough—but unable to make him drink!

We may be able to attract a crowd to a well-advertised service; we may put on an extremely clever and interesting program. But by human endeavor we can never make people intercessors and soul-winners. Only God the Holy Ghost can do that. It is only when the Spirit himself is poured forth into the heart that the Christian can truly say: "There is a love constraining me to go and seek the lost."

When Peter and John were commanded by the Sanhedrin to stop preaching and teaching about Jesus, they exclaimed: "We cannot but speak the things which we have seen and heard" (Acts 4:20).

The Spirit-anointed John Bunyan confessed: "I preached what I *felt*, what I smartingly did *feel*." There will be no lack of happy, eager witnesses for Christ in our churches when believers are filled with the Holy Spirit. The reluctant "Must I?" will be changed to the joyous "May I?"

3. *Irresistible power*

How comforting to the weak, handicapped Christian is the guarantee of the Lord himself that rivers of living water *shall* flow from him when the Holy Ghost takes possession. His power is irresistible; no demons or wicked man can stay its flow. Try to dam up mighty rivers and see what happens! They must have an outlet; a channel must be made for them.

So with the Spirit-filled life. God has promised not only to dwell in us, but also to "walk about" in us (II Cor. 6:16). Not only God in residence in the human soul, but the almighty God in action in a humble believer!

Scientists tell us that there is enough power in a single lump of sugar which, if totally and instantly released, would be sufficient to blow up a city! What, then, is the measure of the power of the Holy Ghost when it flows with divine spontaneity from a sanctified believer? When that same power flowed forth from a hundred and twenty believers on the Day of Pentecost, the hardest city in the world witnessed the greatest revival Jerusalem had ever known. The stoutest barriers were swept away before the living waters that gushed from the Upper Room.

Whatever be our circumstances, however difficult our lot, life in the Holy Ghost will make us irresistible for God. Satan may be allowed to cast us into the fiery furnace, but he is powerless to stop the "Form of the Fourth" from stepping into the furnace along with us.

With the bride in the Song of Solomon, the Spirit-possessed Christian exclaims: "Awake O north wind; and come thou south; blow upon my garden, that the spices thereof may flow out." The biting north wind of adversity or the pleasant south wind of prosperity— all will have the same effect upon the entirely sanctified heart. The sweet spices will flow out for the benefit of others.

4. *The pathway of the Spirit's fulness*

How assuring are the words of Scripture: "This spake he of the Spirit, which they that *believe* [put their trust] in him should receive."

The language of many Christian hearts is this:

> My soul crieth out for the Spirit,
> I'm hungering and thirsting to know
> The fulness of blessing He giveth;
> Now fill me while humbly I bow.

In praying for our Pentecost we must realize that the Holy Ghost does not come according to men's preconceived ideas and plans. He travels along a divinely appointed pathway. It is via the risen and exalted Christ. It is Christ who baptizes with the Holy Ghost. It is He who has received of the Father the promise of the Spirit, so that He might pour Him forth unto men. By the Holy Spirit we are baptized into the mystic body of Christ at our conversion. But it is Jesus alone who baptizes His own people *with* the Holy Spirit.

So Jesus declared: "If any man thirst, let him come unto *me* and drink." In order to be filled with the Holy Spirit, the seeking soul must do three things:

1. Go to Christ direct and ask Him for the coveted blessing. Look away from all else: fix the gaze on the spotless Lamb of God.

2. Go to Him with a *thirsty* heart, longing more than anything else on earth to be filled with the Holy Spirit. It is only those who hunger and thirst after righteousness who are filled. Only the fully consecrated believer can obtain Christ's coronation gift—the gift of the Holy Spirit's fulness.

3. Ask in simple, childlike faith. The Day of Pente-

cost has fully come. There is no longer any need to wait ten days in an upper room. The command to every Christian is to "be filled [*now*] with the Spirit." This word in Ephesians 5:18 is in the present tense. If God commands His children to be filled *now* with the Holy Spirit, then no Christian has the right to remain unfilled one hour after receiving the divine imperative. That being so, then (and we speak reverently) God has no right to withhold from the trusting soul for a single moment what He has commanded it to receive *now*.

In Galatians 3:14 we have the golden key that unlocks the gate into blessing. It reads: "That we might receive the promise of the Spirit through *faith*." God is sovereign, and He has the exclusive right to give whatever outward manifestation of the Spirit is pleasing to Him. "There are diversities of gifts, but the same Spirit. There are diversities of operations, but it is the same God which worketh all in all.... But all these worketh that one and the self-same Spirit, dividing to every man severally as *he will*" (I Cor. 12:4, 6, 11).

Then follow the inevitable questions: "Are all workers of miracles? Have all the gifts of healing? Do all speak with tongues? Do all interpret?" (I Cor. 12:29, 30).

There is but one answer to these questions. It is "No."

Let us leave the outward manifestations to the ordering of a wise God. What we *can* claim, without the slightest fear of being denied, is the incoming of the Holy Spirit himself in response to simple faith. And that is all that really matters: that the blessed Comforter should come into the trusting heart as president—forever afterwards guiding, keeping, and empowering, and revealing to the soul the transcendent beauty of Jesus Christ the Lord.

Then, and then only, will the Christian be fully satisfied. It may well be that just now some reader is earnestly praying:

> Less than Thyself O do not give,
> In might Thyself within me live,
> Come, all Thou hast and art!

Then let that seeking soul take the next decisive step and, resting on the sure promises of God, cry out:

> Holy Ghost, I now receive Thee!
> I accept Thy mighty power:
> And by *faith* I claim Thy promise,
> In this solemn, sacred hour.

---

[1] *The Way to Pentecost*, page 123.

CHAPTER NINE

The Three Baptisms

"I INDEED BAPTIZE YOU with water unto repentance" (Matt. 3:11).

"He shall baptize you with the Holy Ghost and with fire" (Matt. 3:11).

"I have a baptism to be baptized with" (Luke 12: 50).

"Can ye be baptized with the baptism that I am baptized with?" (Mark 10:38).

The New Testament speaks of at least *three* baptisms. This does not contradict Paul's statement in Ephesians that there is "one Lord, one faith, one baptism." Evidently the apostle refers to that unique act of the Holy Spirit whereby penitent sinners become members of the true Church, the mystical Body of Christ.

He brings out the same thought in I Corinthians 12 where he writes: "For by one Spirit, we are all baptized into one body, whether we be Jews or Gentiles." In other words, there is only one baptism that can make us members of the true Church: it is the baptism administered *by* the Holy Ghost himself. It must be distinguished from Christ's act of baptizing His people *with* the Holy Spirit.

Coming back to our texts, we notice that they point to three distinct baptisms.

1. *The baptism of water*

I do not wish to provoke controversy as to the right *mode* of water baptism, whether by sprinkling or immersion. For after all, water baptism, whatever method be used, is but a symbol of the washing away of past transgressions and of the regeneration of the human heart. All over Christendom, with rare exceptions, such as among the Quakers and Salvationists, water baptism is intended to be an outward sign that the baptized person has been admitted into church fellowship and is separated from the old life.

During one of my visits to France I realized this fact as never before. In a memorable service in Paris one Sunday morning, a splendid youth gave his heart to Christ. Although belonging to a Roman Catholic home he had quite frequently attended Pastor Roberts' evangelical church in Rue de Musset. But he had never expressed a desire for baptism in a Protestant church. Shortly after his conversion, however, he was publicly baptized along with other candidates. Pastor Roberts told me that for a Catholic to submit to baptism in an evangelical assembly in France was to publicly announce his admittance into a new church fellowship and his complete severance from Rome. Thus to that youth, water baptism was the most fitting symbol of a spiritual regeneration and renunciation.

2. *The baptism of the Holy Ghost*

This baptism can never be effected by man. Christ alone is able to administer it; for it is He who baptizes with the Holy Ghost and with fire. It is not for sinners, but is the exclusive right of all Christian disciples.

In the record in Acts, of the four outpourings of

the Holy Spirit—upon Jews (chapter 2), Samaritans (chapter 8), Romans (chapter 10), and Greeks (chapter 19)—the recipients in every case were believers in the Lord Jesus. This mighty baptism of fire purges the nature from all carnality and empowers the life for victorious and fruitful service.

The symbol of cloven tongues in the Upper Room, so different from the dove-like appearance of the Spirit at Christ's baptism, confirms Peter's statement in Acts 15:8 and 9, that when God gives the Holy Ghost in Pentecostal measure, He purifies the heart by faith. The promise of Jesus that the baptism of the Spirit would give His disciples power to witness for Him, even in the most difficult places, was abundantly proved on the day of Pentecost. Millions of Christians down the centuries have also found the promise to be true.

Only three simple conditions are laid down for Christians to receive the baptism of the Holy Ghost. They are, first, *prayer* (Luke 11:13); second, *obedience* (Acts 5:32); and third, *faith* (Gal. 3:14).

3. *The baptism of suffering*

This is a mysterious, hallowing process which comes after a personal Pentecost. In the Hebrew economy, it is significant that *after* the Feast of Pentecost and the Blowing of Trumpets came the Feast of Atonement when the children of Israel had to "afflict their souls." This is always the divine order.

Following His Jordan baptism, when the Holy Spirit came upon Him in bodily shape like a dove, Jesus declared that He had yet "a baptism to be baptized with." To the Spirit-anointed Jesus came a mighty baptism of suffering which qualified Him to be the Saviour and Redeemer. "For it became him, for whom are all things, and by whom are all things, in bringing many sons unto glory, to make the captain of their salvation perfect through sufferings. *Though he were a son, yet learned he obedience by the things which he suffered.*" Such a baptism brought forth supplications and prayers with strong crying and tears; yea, it issued in sweat that was like great drops of blood.

The disciple is not above his Master, nor the servant above his Lord. Therefore, every Spirit-baptized Christian qualifies for a baptism of suffering. Let him not shrink from the cup, but let him drink it, bitter though it be, as the portion appointed by a loving, heavenly Father. It is to fit him for closer identification with His Son Jesus Christ that God entirely sanctifies the believer. For it is only "if we suffer" that "we shall also reign with him."

It seems that in these, the closing days of the dispensation of grace, the Lord of the harvest is rapidly ripening His grain. To prepare the bridehood saints to meet their heavenly Bridegroom Jesus Christ, the Father is sending dark, dusky sorrow in increasing measure. In Korea, China, Russia and other lands, the people of God are wading to glory through seas of great tribulation. In the measure that they can receive it, God will honor His children everywhere with the fellowship of Christ's sufferings.

The crowns of the saints are cast in crucibles; scars are the price of their sceptres. That they might occupy exalted places in the Kingdom age, the Lord takes His chosen ones deep into the valley of humiliation. Let us then take courage as we enter our baptism of suffering. "Our light affliction, which is but for a moment, worketh for us a far more exceeding and eternal weight of glory."

"Out of the presses of pain
Cometh the soul's best wine,
And the eyes that have shed no rain
Can shed but little shine."

Many years ago, at a Bible conference in Battersea, London, an old saint sat next to me at the dining table. Pointing to the first chapter of the Philippian Epistle, he read the words: "For unto you it is given in the behalf of Christ, not only to believe on him, but also to suffer for his sake."

Then he emphasized the truth that suffering, when in the will of God, is as much a *gift* as salvation itself.

That old warrior was God's messenger to a young man who had not long been sanctified wholly. Until that memorable table talk he had known little, if any, of the third baptism. That honor was reserved for later days.

It makes all the difference when the Spirit-filled child of God can believe that crushing sorrow and bitter disappointment are agents in the omnipotent hand of the Father to perfect the work of grace in his soul and fit him for greater usefulness in the kingdom. A discerning disciple has aptly said:

"I walked a mile with Pleasure,
She chattered all the way,
But left me none the wiser
For all she had to say.
I walked a mile with Sorrow,
And never a word said she.
But oh, the things I learned from her
When Sorrow walked with me."

The long summer sun "smites its burning into the grain and turns it to sweetness." So, for the child of God, fierce trial is "the burning of his Father's sunshine." The golden grain of harvest is bound to follow.

CHAPTER TEN

Emblems of the Spirit—The Dove and the Dew

IN HIS CONDESCENDING GOODNESS God often speaks
to men in symbolic language.

Unaided by the Holy Spirit, men's finite minds
can never grasp the immensities of the infinite. Therefore many important Bible truths are illuminated by
emblems or symbols. Our Lord Jesus used this method
in much of His teaching. He selected such emblems
as lilies, sparrows, sheep, gold, salt, and eye salve, etc.,
to illustrate the deep things of His kingdom.

In like manner the character and ministry of the
Holy Spirit are sometimes set forth in emblematic
form. Six emblems of the Holy Ghost in Scripture
are: the dove, the dew, air, breath or wind, fire, and
oil.

The Dove

This emblem of the Holy Spirit is first in our list
because it is seen in the opening chapter of Genesis.
In verse two we read that the Spirit of God moved
("brooded") over the dark, chaotic waters of the deep.

The word "moved" is rendered "incubatat" in the
Vulgate version, while in Deuteronomy 32:11 the same
word is translated "fluttereth." Thus we have in this

"moving" of the Spirit in Genesis 1 the picture of a mother dove brooding over her nest and nourishing her young. Referring to this same word, the scholarly, Gesenius said it is "figuratively used of the Spirit of God, who *brooded* over the shapeless mass of the earth, cherishing and vivifying." Our own Milton expressed it thus:

> ... O Spirit. Thou from the first
> Wast present, and with mighty wing outspread
> Dove-like sat'st brooding on the vast abyss,
> And madest it pregnant.

Later in Genesis we see the part played by a dove in the tragic story of the Flood. Twenty centuries of work had been submerged and millions of rebellious sinners swept into eternity. Then Noah sent out a dove from the ark. But that gentle bird (unlike the raven) found no rest for her feet on the troubled waters of judgment. Only when the flood waters had subsided and the work of purification was complete did the dove find rest upon the earth. How like the Holy Spirit this is, as we shall see later.

Coming to the New Testament we find the dove appearing at the river Jordan, when Jesus was baptized with water. Luke tells us that "Jesus also being baptized, and praying, the heaven was opened, and the Holy Ghost descended in a bodily shape like a dove upon him" (Luke 3:21, 22).

The characteristics of the dove are well known. That gentle bird is noted for its purity, love, fidelity and peaceableness. Jesus, when sending forth His disciples, told them to be as "harmless as doves." This indicates the peaceful nature of the dove. Other birds rely mainly on their claws or talons in times of conflict. But the dove depends upon its amazing speed and

swiftly soars above the strife of battle. It is the bird
of peace.

When the Holy Spirit fills the human heart, He takes
from it all carnal desires for strife and division. The
blessed Comforter never finds rest in a combatative
and backbiting spirit. The coveted fruit of perfect peace
never grows on the tree of self-will and carnal assertive-
ness. In the realm of grace it is true that even now the
meek inherit the earth.

There is a tragedy about the gifts of the Holy Spirit
which does not enter into the sphere of fruitbearing.
Strange though it may be, it is true that wonderful gifts,
such as prophecy, faith, knowledge and tongues, may
still be exercised even when the fulness of the Spirit
has gone from the heart.

For, said Paul, we may have all these outward
supernatural manifestations and yet be destitute of
divine love (Greek: *agape*). No man is without divine
love if he is filled with the Holy Ghost: for the fruit
of the Spirit is love. Yes, and the love of God is *shed
abroad* in our hearts when the Holy Ghost is reigning
within. Some Christians are in danger of using the very
gifts of the Spirit in the same way many women wear
their jewelry—to draw attention to themselves. When
that happens, the gentle Holy Spirit is grieved and
withdraws His fulness from the heart. Then perfect
peace is replaced by pride of place and carnal disput-
ings. How fitting is the prayer of Dr. Reed:

> Come as the Dove, and spread Thy wings,
>   The wings of *peaceful* love;
> And let Thy Church on earth become
>   Bless'd as the Church above.

We may exercise wonderful gifts when still in a
carnal state. But we can never bring forth the fruits

of the Holy Spirit unless the Comforter himself is in control of our whole being.

Unlike most other birds, the dove has no bag of gall. Its purity is rare. The ancient naturalists considered gall as being a source and fountain of contention. They supposed that the bitterness of the gall infused itself into the spirit. Be that as it may, of one thing we can be sure. It is that the Spirit of God is absolutely pure and knows nothing of sinful sourness. So in the life that is fully yielded to the Spirit's gracious control there is true holiness of character. And that is the paramount need in the Christian Church today.

> Spirit of Holiness, do Thou
> Dwell in this soul of mine;
> Possess my heart and make me know
> A sanctity divine.

Many birds are like some Hollywood stars—they mate very frequently! But not so with the faithful dove. It is strictly monogamous and never desires another mate. Such fidelity in a bird is something rarely found in humans today. This faithful affection beautifully portrays the character of the Holy Spirit. Jesus promised His disciples: "I will pray the Father, and he shall send you another Comforter, that he may *abide* with you for ever" (John 14:16).

Here indeed is transcendent fidelity—that God the Holy Ghost should take frail creatures of dust into eternal partnership with himself!

This means that a Spirit-filled believer is never left alone to meet the trials of life. Not for a single moment will the Comforter desert the trusting heart. Through all the changing circumstances of our earthly pilgrimage—in joy and in sorrow, in poverty and in plenty, in sickness and in health, in youth and in old age—there is the firm guarantee of His glorious presence. The blessed Holy Ghost never "squeezes us dry" and then throws us away, as some people do with an orange or lemon! The trusting heart can always count on the Holy Ghost to "see him through." Hallelujah!

Yes, and the trusting heart of the Spirit-filled Christian will display that fidelity and steadfastness of purpose which earns the coveted commendation from the Master: "Well done, thou good and *faithful* servant: enter thou into the joy of thy Lord."

It is the special work of the Holy Spirit to make us both good and faithful. But faithful love is bound to suffer. In fact, real love is inseparable from pain. All parents know this to be true, as they sorrow over departed or wayward loved ones.

The dove is not only the bird of peace, purity, and loving fidelity; it is also a bird of sorrow. Its plaintive notes have more sadness in them than the voice of other birds. The lonely dove as it coos for its lost mate and mourns for its scattered brood has an unforgettable pathos in its tone.

And so the faithful, loving Holy Spirit can be grieved (Eph. 4:30). Away back in Old Testament days we read that Israel "vexed his Holy Spirit" (Isa. 63:10).

The Holy Spirit is the passionate Lover of the Lord Jesus. He delights to glorify the Lamb of God, and He works with tireless zeal to bring in that day when the kingdoms of this world shall become the kingdoms of the Lord Jesus Christ. It grieves His tender heart when humans dishonor Christ and when believers live and talk as if they were worldlings.

There is a very illuminating passage in the epistle of James, chapter 4, which has been unhappily translated in the Authorized Version: "The spirit that dwelleth in us lusteth to envy." The more correct translation (given in The Amplified New Testament) is this: "The Spirit Whom He hath caused to dwell in us yearns over us with a jealous love." Here is the picture of the Holy Spirit's love for us, which is so intense that it is rightly jealous lest we share our affections with the world.

Therefore, the preceding verse in James 4 is a solemn warning to all Christians: "Know ye not that the friendship of the world is enmity with God?" This grief of the Holy Spirit finds an echo in the heart of the truly sanctified believer. Like Paul he yearns to know not only the power of Christ's resurrection but also the fellowship of His sufferings. Thus, as he walks in close obedience to the Holy Spirit, he feels within his soul from time to time those "groanings" of the Spirit "which cannot be uttered."

Carnal Christians do not come within a thousand miles of such divinely mystical experiences. Such heights (or should we say depths?) in the Spirit-filled life are not traversed by the shallow-minded professor of religion.

To be conformed to the image of Christ means that we have given up the right to ourselves. In fact, we are "delivered unto death for Jesus' sake" (II Cor. 4:11).

Abandonment to the Holy Ghost is the grand secret of conformity to the image of Christ. For the Comforter is the only One who can make us like Jesus.

The Dew

In the little church where I found Christ as my Saviour they often sang Mrs. C. H. Morris' beautiful hymn on the Holy Spirit. One of its verses breathes out this prayer:

Come like dew from heaven falling,
Come like spring's refreshing shower;
Holy Ghost, for Thee we're calling,
Come in all Thy quickening power.

Among the many gracious promises of God is that
in Hosea 14:5, "I will be as the *dew* unto Israel." This
lovely emblem of the Holy Spirit is attractively rele-
vant in these days of noise and tension. The tempo of
modern life is so fierce that everywhere people are
cracking up under the strain.

A Japanese doctor once told Stanley Jones, the
famous missionary, that tuberculosis is no longer killer
No. 1 in his country. It is now heart disease and high
blood pressure, he said. Asked for the reason, he replied: "Spiritual uneasiness."

The spectacle of Christless multitudes tossed on the
waves of fear and folly is tragic enough. But sadder
still is the sight of Christians who are not enjoying
their birthright of inward serenity and peace. They
lack the freshness and fragrance of souls who are
sparkling with the dew of the Holy Spirit.

Some folk mistake the click of religious machinery
for spiritual activity. They often think the energy and
glitter of human enthusiasm to be the power of the
Holy Ghost. They fail to discern between the psychic
and the spiritual. They seem to forget that most of
nature's majestic movements are silent. The break of
dawn, the shining of stars, the blooming of flowers,
and the revolving of earth upon its axis—all are silent
but irresistible.

Of course the Holy Ghost can come as the sound
of a rushing mighty wind. He did so at Pentecost. He
may be found amid the earthquake and the fire. It
has been my privilege to be in prayer meetings that
beggar description. They were times when heavenly

gales so swept over the kneeling worshippers that with
one voice they cried aloud and shouted the praises of
the Most High God. Carnal and critical observers
might have likened them to men drunk with wine.
They would not have known it was the exhilaration
of the Holy Spirit that gave such unbounded joy and
vocal expression.

But the Holy Spirit may come also in power as
the gentle dew and in the still small voice. John Green-
leaf Whittier, the Quaker poet, expressed the longing
of a host of Christians when he prayed:

> Drop Thy still dews of quietness
> Till all our strivings cease,
> Take from our souls the strain and stress,
> And let our ordered lives confess
> The beauty of Thy peace.

The blessing of dew was a much-coveted bestowment in Palestine where, for months at a time, no rain
falls and the ground becomes parched through the prolonged heat of the sun. The patriarch Isaac in blessing
his son Jacob said: "God give thee of the dew of heav-
en" (Gen. 27:28).

The blessing of the Lord upon the saints as they
dwell together in unity is likened unto the dew upon
the mountains of Zion (Ps. 133).

Thus the emblem of dew portrays the refreshing
and fertilizing power of the Holy Spirit in the soul
that is fully yielded to Him.

The formation of nature's dew is an object lesson
in the rare art of receiving the coveted dew of the
Holy Spirit. In the silence of the night the sparkling
drops gather according to a well-defined law. First,
there must be the shining of the sun upon the earth
during the previous day. For a dewy morning comes
only after the warming of the earth by the sun. Then

follows the radiation of that heat into the surrounding atmosphere during the night. What the earth has received from the heavens is given back into the waiting night air. The incumbent atmosphere becomes so saturated with moisture that, unable by the contact of differing temperatures to retain that moisture any longer, it distils it upon leaf, flower and grass in myriad dew-drops.

The earth must both receive and then return the heat given by the sun if it is to be rewarded with refreshing dew. Hard, unresponsive soil receives no such recompense. A walk through the garden on a summer's morning will often present a startling contrast. On the tender grass, leaf, and fragrant flowers can be seen the dew drops, glittering like precious diamonds. Yet, not far away, on the hard paths or barren spots, no such sparkling dew appears.

This is surely a parable of human life.

Proud and stubborn hearts never sparkle with heavenly dew. It is only the humble and tender-hearted Christian, opening every avenue of his being to the shining rays of the Sun of righteousness, who glistens with the graces of the Holy Spirit. Warmed by the indwelling Comforter, he then gives out to others, in thankful service and radiant testimony, of the rich blessings he has received from heaven. Then, in the silence and quietness of the "morning watch," he waits upon the Lord for the promised refreshment and renewal of strength. And according to divine law, it never fails to come (Isa. 40:31; 58:10, 11).

> The air surrounding thee is full of God,
> With love and life and blessing for thee stored;
> Get cool and quiet and the dew will fall—
> A little at a time, not once for all.

Another striking feature of dew formation is that, provided there are no clouds in the sky, then the hotter the night, the more plentiful the supply of dew in the morning. So it is with the Spirit's mysterious and wonderful operations. Sin clouds between the soul and God will prevent the gentle dew from falling. But if the sky is clear and communion with the Lord is unbroken by disobedience, then the hotter the trials and testings of life, the more abundant will be the supply of heavenly grace.

> He giveth more grace when the burdens grow greater,
> He sendeth more strength when the labours increase,
> To added affliction, He addeth His mercy,
> To multiplied trials, He multiplies peace.

CHAPTER ELEVEN

Emblems of the Spirit—Air, Fire, Water, Oil

Air, wind or breath

THIS IS A BIBLE symbol which often denotes the life-giving, regenerating power of the Holy Spirit.

Invisible and mysterious like the wind, yet irresistible in its force, is the operation of the Spirit of God.

The late Dr. F. E. Marsh used to relate the story of a skeptic who told a certain Christian that he did not believe there was a Holy Spirit simply because he had never seen Him. So he thus questioned the saint:

"Have you ever seen the Holy Spirit?"

"No."

"Have you ever tasted the Holy Spirit?"

"No."

"Have you ever smelled the Holy Spirit?"

"No."

"Have you ever felt the Holy Spirit?"

"*Yes.*"

Turning on his critic, the man of God said: "Now let me ask you a question or two: Have you ever seen a pain?"

"No."

"Have you ever tasted a pain?"

"No."

"Have you ever smelled a pain?"

"No."

"Have you ever *felt* a pain?"

"Yes."

"So," said the Christian, "I have *felt* the power of the Holy Spirit."

Elihu the Buzite once said to Job: "The Spirit of God hath made me, and the *breath* of the Almighty hath given me life" (Job 33:3).

Elihu thus symbolized the life-giving power of the Holy Spirit by the figure of *breath*.

In his vision, Ezekiel the prophet saw a valley of dry bones—a huge graveyard. He was then commanded by God to prophesy unto the dry bones: "Thus saith the Lord God unto these bones: Behold, I will cause *breath* to enter into you, and ye shall live" (ch. 37:1–5).

There followed a great shaking of the bones and the clothing of them with sinews, flesh and skin. But even then they were but an army of corpses! Movement, noise, and the rattling bones were not enough. Vibrant life was missing.

So Ezekiel cried out: "Come from the four winds, O *breath*, and breathe upon these slain, that they may live." Then came the vital breath from the heavens—and the miracle took place! "They *lived*," and stood up upon their feet, an exceeding great army" (vss. 9, 10).

God then explained to Ezekiel the meaning of the amazing vision and prophecy. He declared: "Behold, O my people . . . ye shall know that I am the Lord, when I have brought you up out of your graves, and shall put my Spirit in you, and ye shall *live*" (ch. 37:12–14).

It was the coming of the Holy Spirit as wind or breath which alone could bring up the nation Israel from the dead, and give its people life and vitality.

Our crying need of today is the descent of God's almighty wind—the Holy Spirit. We have plenty of preaching, the constant click of religious machinery, and well-nigh perfect organization. But, alas, there is so little of divine life in our churches. Virile, Spirit-transformed men and women seem so few in our midst.

Oh for that inspired, prophetic voice of prayer that will bring again the Breath from heaven upon the graveyard of Christendom!

> "O Breath of God, breathe on us now,
> And move within us while we pray;
> The spring of our new life art Thou,
> The very light of our new day."
>
> —A. H. Vine

Fire

This symbol sets forth the purifying, penetrating and energizing power of the Holy Ghost.

In his Apocalypse, the apostle John saw in heaven "seven lamps of fire burning before the throne, which are the seven Spirits of God" (Rev. 4:5).

This figure does not mean that there are seven Holy Spirits. The number seven in Scripture is often the mark of perfection or completeness. Thus, in symbolic language, the Holy Spirit in His plentitude is likened unto seven lamps of burning fire.

Isaiah, under divine inspiration, called the Holy Spirit the "Spirit of burning" (Isa. 4:4).

On that unique Day of Pentecost recorded in Acts, chapter two, we see that the emblem of the Holy Ghost was not wind but "cloven tongues like as of fire." It was the roaring of the divine fire that gave a "*sound*" as of rushing wind. The outstanding symbol on that great day was *fire*. For what purpose? To thoroughly purify and mightily empower Christian men and women who already possessed the breath of eternal life. Some days before Pentecost Jesus had breathed upon His disciples, and said unto them: "Receive ye the Holy Ghost" (John 20:22). Those same disciples returned from Olivet after Christ's Ascension, with unmistakable marks of the new birth upon them. We are told that "they worshipped him and returned to Jerusalem with great joy: and were continually in the temple praising and blessing God" (Luke 24:52, 53). But in spite of all this, the disciples had to tarry until they were endued with power from on high.

It was the *fire* of the Holy Ghost that burned up the dross of carnal pride and fear, and gave the hundred-and-twenty a supernatural power which shook the hardest city in the world and brought three thousand sinners to Christ in a single day.

Well wrote Samuel Chadwick: "The supreme need of the Church is fire. The one persistent prayer of them that 'cry and sigh' is for the fiery baptism of Pentecost. . . . The baptism of the Spirit is the baptism of fire. Spirit-filled souls are ablaze for God. They love with a love that glows. They believe with a faith that kindles. They serve with a devotion that consumes. They hate sin with a fierceness that burns." [1]

The Great Plague of London in 1665 wiped out one-seventh of the city's population. About 60,000 people out of 450,000 died of the all-conquering cholera. Medical science was powerless to arrest the awful march of death in the stricken metropolis. Then came the Great Fire of London, which penetrated deep into both houses and land and thoroughly purged away the deadly plague. The fever fled before the fire.

And so sin, in all its subtle, persistent forms, is

banished when the fire of the Holy Ghost does its work
in the human heart.

> "To burn up every trace of sin,
> To bring the light and glory in,
> The revolution now begin,
> Send the Fire!"

So sang William Booth and his early Salvationists.
England and the world felt the purifying and ennobling
glow of their Pentecostal fire.

Water

Again and again in Scripture water is mentioned
as a beautiful emblem of the Spirit. It refers not only
to His cleansing efficacy, but also to His strengthening,
healing and fructifying powers. Water purifies. It also
fertilizes. These wonderful qualities are clearly brought
out in the following passages:

Isaiah 44:3, 4—"I will pour water upon him that
is thirsty, and floods upon the dry ground: I will pour
out my Spirit upon thy seed, and my blessing upon
thine offspring. And they shall spring up as among the
grass, as willows by the water courses."

Ezekiel 36:25, 27, 29, 30—"Then will I sprinkle
clean water upon you, and ye shall be clean: from all
your filthiness, and from all your idols, will I cleanse
you. And I will put my Spirit within you, and cause
you to walk in my statutes.... And I will call for the
corn, and will increase it. And I will multiply the fruit
of the tree, and the increase of the field."

John 7:38, 39—"Out of his belly [inner being]
shall flow rivers of living water. This spake he of
the Spirit, which they that believe on him should receive."

In these Scriptures is the glorious picture of the

purity, plentitude, and power which come from the bountiful hand of the Holy Spirit.

God wants us to be free from sin in order that we might be filled with fruit. "But now being made free from sin ... ye have your fruit unto holiness" (Rom. 6:22). First the cleansing, then the fertility. The Lord desires His children to be fruitful. Barrenness is repulsive to Him, and brings the reproach that fell upon the fig tree when it failed to satisfy the Master's hunger long ago (Mark 11:12–14).

To His disciples Jesus said: "Herein is my Father glorified, that ye bear much fruit" (John 15:8).

Fruitbearing is not the result of self-effort; it comes only as we abide in Christ and He in us. And such a life of constant abiding is only possible as we are filled with the Spirit.

When does the wilderness become a fruitful field? The answer is plain: It is when "the Spirit is poured upon us from on high" (Isa. 32:15).

The fruit of the Spirit is love, joy, peace, longsuffering, gentleness, goodness, faith, meekness, self-control (Gal. 5:22, 23).

Voltaire, the famous French skeptic, was asked if he knew of anybody who could compare with Jesus Christ. He answered: "I once met John Fletcher" (of Madeley). The Spirit-filled Fletcher had a soul like a well-watered garden. Its luscious fruit was tasted and enjoyed even by the anti-clerical Voltaire.

Oil

As yet another symbol of the Holy Spirit, oil speaks of that equipment for service, that bestowment of wisdom, illumination and knowledge, which is the portion of those whose hearts are pure and whose lives are fully possessed by the Paraclete.

In ancient Israel the prophets, kings and priests were always anointed with oil before undertaking their sacred office. Of David we read that when "Samuel took the horn of oil, and anointed him in the presence of his brethren"; then "the Spirit of the Lord came upon David from that day forward" (I Sam. 16:13).

A relic of that age-long ceremony is seen at the coronation of British royalty. When our beloved Queen Elizabeth II was crowned Queen in Westminster Abbey, much of that unique ceremony was seen by millions of people on television. But the most sacred part of that royal drama was hidden from all but those privileged people who were near the throne. It was not televised because of its hallowed nature. It was the anointing of the Queen with oil by the Archbishop of Canterbury. Upon her head, the palms of her hands, and upon her breast was placed the anointing oil. It betokened the grace of the Holy Spirit, which alone could fit our monarch to perform her special task.

At the consecration of Israel's High Priest, the anointing with oil came after he had been washed with water (Ex. 29:4–7). In like manner, it is only those who have been sanctified and cleansed "with the washing of water by the word" who can claim the anointing divine for the service of the Master. Just as oil makes a man's "face to shine" (Ps. 104:15), so does the anointing of the Holy Spirit give to the Christian special illumination and understanding in the things of God.

In these latter days, when subtle heresy abounds, and the love of many believers is waxing cold, we need that anointing of the Spirit which abides and which "teaches us of all things" (I John 2:27).

All we require in Christian service, on the path from earth to heaven, is provided for us in the Holy Ghost. Let us press our claim for the inheritance. He who

purchased it with the price of His own precious blood
will gladly shed forth the Holy Ghost in our hearts if
we but trust and obey.

-----

[1] *The Way to Pentecost*, pages 43, 96

CHAPTER TWELVE

The Gifts of the Spirit—
Faith, Healing, and Miracles

GOD WANTS HIS CHILDREN to be well instructed about the gifts of the Holy Spirit. Paul made this clear when he declared: "Now concerning spiritual gifts, brethren, I would not have you ignorant" (I Cor. 12:1). In view of such an admonition it is folly for any Christians to despise or oppose this delicate but important theme.

That balanced Bible teacher, President Jared F. Gerig, has rightly said: "A clear understanding of the 'gifts of the Spirit' is vital to the doctrines of the Church and of the Holy Spirit." He further declared: "We must acknowledge that the various gifts are needed today, and that they are in existence to meet that need. When the Holy Ghost is allowed to have His way, an examination of a cross section of the Church will find all these gifts in operation. In fact, the Church is effective only as the various gifts are recognized and given opportunity for manifestation." [1]

Some of our good brethren in the Holiness Movements need to ponder such frank and challenging words, coming as they do from an acknowledged scholar of the Wesleyan persuasion.

Dr. Jared Gerig has but echoed the wise words of John Wesley, who wrote: "By reflecting on an odd book which I had read, I was fully convinced of what I had long suspected. (1) That the Montanists, in the second and third centuries, were real, scriptural Christians, and (2) that the grand reason why the miraculous gifts were so soon withdrawn was not only that faith and holiness were well nigh lost, but that dry, formal, orthodox men began then to ridicule whatever gifts they had not themselves and to decry them all as either madness or imposture." (Works: Vol. 2, page 204)

George Matheson paid a deserving compliment to the early followers of Wesley when he called Montanism "the Methodism of the second century."

Well might Dr. Frank B. Stanger (president of Asbury Theological Seminary) be concerned about the attitude of the present-day Holiness groups to the operations of the Holy Spirit. He writes: "This is the question that haunts me, and I must share it with you: Is the contemporary Holiness Movement being true to its genius as a movement of the Spirit?" [2]

He believes that one of the perils besetting "the Church of the Spirit" is spiritual indolence. He goes on to say: "The antidote to spiritual complacency is found in a valid and practical use of the gifts of the Spirit." [3] He concludes his splendid paper with these words: "Thank God for the Gift of the Spirit, the gifts of the Spirit, the fruit of the Spirit, the commission of the Spirit."

The greatest discourse on the gifts of the Holy Spirit is recorded in I Corinthians 12 to 14. Seeing it is part of a church epistle, there can be no doubt that its teaching is as valid today as it was in the early Corinthian assembly.

The nine gifts or manifestations of the Spirit mentioned by Paul in I Corinthians 12:7-10 can be divided into three groups: (1) the "power" gifts of faith, miracles, and healing; (2) the gifts relating to divine revelation, viz., the word of wisdom, the word of knowledge, the discerning of spirits; (3) gifts for the purposes of worship. They are prophecy, tongues, and the interpretation of tongues.

It is evident that the miraculous gifts of the Holy Spirit did not cease at the close of the apostolic age. As the *Encyclopaedia Britannica* has pointed out, miracles, healing, and the glossolalia recurred "in Christian revivals of every age, e.g., among the mendicant friars of the 13th century, among the Jansenists and early Quakers, the persecuted Protestants of the Cevennes," [4] and among many other groups of Spirit-filled believers.

To meet the awful need in these latter days of gross materialism and "higher criticism" we must, like Paul of old, "make the Gentiles obedient by word and deed, through mighty signs and wonders, by the power of the Spirit of God" (Rom. 15:18, 19).

We are challenged by Communist and Moslem alike to give convincing evidence that Jesus Christ is not in the tomb, but is alive forever more and that He still works wonders on earth, as He did in the days of His flesh.

The gifts of faith, healing, and miracles need defining.

The gift of faith, mentioned in I Corinthians 12:9, must be distinguished from that saving faith which everybody must exercise in Christ in order to be a Christian. It is different, also, from faith as a *fruit* of the Spirit which *all* "born-again" souls manifest. All Christians have not the *gift* of faith, which is a special bestowment of the Holy Ghost upon certain of God's servants at times of crisis and great need. Weymouth translates I Corinthians 12:9: "To a third man, by means of the same Spirit, *special* faith."

This Spirit-bestowed gift of faith is certainly a "power" gift and is often linked up with the working of miracles and healing. In fact, some of the older theologians called this special quality of faith the "faith of miracles." Two Bible examples of men who, in times of great need, were given by God this gift of special faith, are Elijah and Paul.

Elijah's calm confidence on Carmel, when surrounded by hundreds of false prophets and a host of backslidden Israelites, betokened a special quality of faith.

So sure was he that God would instantly answer his own prayer for supernatural fire, that he even taunted his opponents because of their helpless Baal (I Kings 18:24–39).

The apostle Paul evidently exercised this gift of faith during and after the great storm in the Mediterranean (Acts 27). He counselled the terrified crew: "Be of good cheer: for I *believe* God, that it shall be even as it was told me!"

Paul had a God-given confidence that not a life on board would be lost. That faith lived on even when the ship was wrecked and when both crew and passengers had to flee from the boat and make their way through violent seas to the shore. Yes, and that faith was triumphant. Thus we read: "And so it came to pass that they all escaped safe to land" (Acts 27:44).

In modern times we have George Muller of Bristol as an example of a man who on many occasions exercised the gift of faith. The astonishing record of his accomplishments for God prove that he repeatedly received from the Holy Spirit a special quality of faith.

This gift of faith is badly needed in our assemblies today. In the hands of humble, truly sanctified Christians it could have far-reaching results in the Kingdom of God. Certainly in every scripturally constituted church (which is the "Body of Christ" in that community: read I Corinthians 12:27) there should be earnest prayer that at least one member would receive the *gift* of faith.

The gift of healing (more correctly termed "gifts of healings": I Cor. 12:28) was used by our Lord right throughout His public ministry. From the commencing days in Galilee, when He went about "healing all manner of sickness" (Matt. 4:23), until He came to Malchus in the Garden of Gethsemane and "touched his ear, and healed him" (Luke 22:51), Jesus manifested the power and willingness of God to heal the sick.

This wonderful gift was also in marked evidence in the early church, and proved of great value in the spread of the Gospel. When Æneas was healed of the palsy under the ministry of Peter, "all that dwelt at Lydda and Saron saw him, and turned to the Lord" (Acts 9:33–35).

In the 17th century the ministry of George Fox the Quaker was sealed of God by several cases of healing. The dying Baptist woman in Baldock, Hertfordshire, the sickly Edward Pyort in Totnes, Devonshire, and the woman in Bishoprick who could neither eat nor speak, were among those who were gloriously healed. (The *Journal of George Fox*: A Revised Text edited by Norman Penny: pages 92, 114, 116.)

In the nineteenth century marvellous cures were effected in Europe. Saintly Dorothy Trudel in the Swiss village of Mannedorf, and godly Pastor Blumhart in the heart of the Black Forest in Germany, witnessed glorious scenes of divine healing. People flocked to these centers of spiritual power from various parts of Europe, and many hundreds of souls were brought to Christ in consequence.

It was the writer's privilege to see genuine cases of healing during pioneer revival campaigns in the north of England from 1931 to 1940, under the auspices of the International Holiness Mission and the Calvary Holiness Church. Such demonstrations of supernatural power were potent factors in the raising up of virile Full Salvation assemblies in Britain.

Great care must be taken to *guard against fanaticism* concerning the gift of healing. Some people have mistakenly thought that those who possessed this gift would be able to cure all and sundry. But such was not the case even in our Lord's ministry. It is true that in certain places He healed all who were brought to Him. But in other places, such as Nazareth and the Pool of Bethesda (Mark 6:5; John 5:3–9), only a few out of many sick folk were healed by Him.

With the apostle Paul the same thing happened. Writing to Timothy he stated plainly: "Trophimus have I left at Miletum sick" (II Tim. 4:20). Why did he not exercise the gift of healing (which undoubtedly he possessed) on behalf of Trophimus on that occasion? We don't know the answer.

One thing is sure, however. Whenever the prayer of faith is offered, the sick are healed (James 5:15). But there are times when even the most devout saints are not able to pray with real assurance for the deliverance of the sick. Paul himself had this experience when pleading earnestly for the removal of his "thorn in the flesh." He received an answer from the Lord, but it was a gracious "No," accompanied by a promise of abundant grace (II Cor. 12:7–9).

It would seem that the safest and wisest way in the ministry of divine healing is for both the minister and the seekers to quietly and unhurriedly wait upon the Lord for clear guidance before hands are laid upon the sick.

Then the Lord, by the Holy Spirit, will either give us His own faith for the healing of the sick or else restrain us from claiming bodily cures.

Unfortunately much confusion and frustration have occurred in public revival and healing campaigns through an almost mechanical process of "laying on" of hands. Unfortunately sufferers have been "keyed up" to expect instant deliverance without having been first instructed carefully in the laws of spiritual and physical healing.

When the Lord quietly pours His own faith into our waiting hearts, then there comes an assurance of healing which never fails. This I have proved to be true on many occasions. In the case of the miraculous healing of the lame man at the Beautiful gate of the temple, Peter declared that it was "the faith which is *by him* [Christ]" which brought deliverance to the cripple (Acts 4:16).

It must also be stressed that the true gifts of healing mentioned in I Corinthians 12:9 are not mere psychic operations such as often occur in so-called Christian Science circles. Many of their cures are the result of mind over matter and must not be confused with those manifestations of healing which are the direct infusion of the Holy Spirit through His sanctified children.

The working of miracles (I Cor. 12:10) can be allied to, and also distinct from, the gifts of healings. The literal Greek of the passage is "operations of works of power" (*dunamis*). There are miracles of healing mentioned in Scripture, such as the instantaneous deliverance of the cripple at the temple gate (Acts 3:2–8). In the next chapter, verse 4, we read: "For the man was above forty years old, on whom this *miracle of healing* was shewed."

But there are other miracles referred to which are

distinct from bodily healing. Examples are: (1) The turning of water into wine (John 2:1–11), performed by Jesus; (2) the feeding of the five thousand (John 6:5–14), performed by Jesus; (3) walking on the sea (Matt. 14:24–27), performed by Jesus; (4) increase of the widow's oil (II Kings 4:1–7), performed by Elisha; (5) raising of Dorcas from the dead (Acts 9:36–41), performed by Peter; (6) deliverance from a venomous snake (Acts 28:3–6), performed by Paul.

Outside Bible times there have been authenticated miracles wrought in the power of the Holy Ghost by humble saints. An undoubted miracle of healing was wrought by George Fox when he visited Hawkshead (North England) in 1653. Entering a certain home he saw there "a boy lying in a cradle which they rocked, about eleven years old. And he was grown almost double." Fox records: "Then was I moved by the Lord God to lay my hands upon him and speak to him, and so bid the lass take him again and put on his clothes." The helpless crippled boy was instantly delivered.

Said the mother of the boy to George Fox some years later: "Presently, after you were gone, we came home and found our son playing in the streets." The lad grew to be "a straight, full youth. . . . So the Lord have the praise." (*Journal*, pages 92–93)

Then there is the record of the raising of the dead by John Welch, the outstanding Scottish prayer-warrior of the sixteenth century. The miracle is related in that interesting volume, *Scots Worthies*, edited by Dr. Andrew Bonar. It took place during Welch's stay in France, and the person concerned was a young noble-man, the heir of Lord Ochiltree, governor of Edinburgh Castle. This youth had lain dead for over forty-eight hours. In fact, the doctors made a thorough examina-tion of the corpse, even severely pinching the the body with pinchers and buffeting the head with a twisted bowspring, before finally pronouncing him stark dead.

Then in answer to the prolonged wrestling of praying John Welch, the young nobleman was raised to life, to the amazement of the onlookers.

In these latter days of satanic power and "lying wonders" the saints do well to prayerfully watch against seducing spirits that would drive them into fanaticism and hysteria. But to rule out the probability of New-Testament-like miracles on the eve of Christ's return is to shut one's eyes to Bible prediction and divine power.

That God will "shew wonders in the heavens and *in the earth* before the great and terrible day of the Lord come" (Joel 2:30, 31) is sufficient warrant for high expectancy. The Holy Ghost will again give His answer to every argument of Satan. He is pledged to present to the heavenly Bridegroom at His second coming, a Bride fully panoplied with spiritual graces and gifts.

---

1 *Insights into Holiness* (Beacon Hill Press, Kansas City) pp. 223–224
2 *Further Insights into Holiness*, p. 223.
3 *Ibid.*, p. 225
4 *11th Edition, Vol. 27*, pp. 9–10

CHAPTER THIRTEEN

The Gifts of the Spirit——The Word of Wisdom, The Word of Knowledge, Discerning of Spirits

The word of wisdom

"FOR TO ONE IS GIVEN by the Spirit the word of wisdom" (I Cor. 12:8), heads the list of the miraculous manifestations of the Holy Spirit mentioned in I Corinthians 12. Its prominent position may well be due to its necessary use in the guarding and controlling of many of the other gifts as they operate in the church.

Much disrepute has come to the cause of Christ through the extravagances and the unwise zeal of Christians who have exercised the gifts of prophecy, healing, and tongues, etc. The "word of wisdom," which is indeed a word in season, would have saved much heartache and misunderstanding in the past. We need it badly for present and future occasions.

The gift of the "word of wisdom" is something entirely different from that natural wisdom with which some people are endowed. Significantly it is called a *word* of wisdom. This means it is a special *utterance* of supernatural wisdom, given by the Holy Spirit to the believer, so that he might reveal to the Church the "deep things of God."

We agree with Dr. J. Massie that such teaching of divine truth appeals to the intuitional faculty. It brings to the heart an unveiling of truth which, although intuitive, is also assuring.

Then again, this supernatural gift of the word of wisdom is especially valuable in times when important decisions and vital problems face the Church of God. How often have we found, in perplexing circumstances, after much discussion with Christian brethren, that suddenly the longed for "word of wisdom" was spoken by one of the company present. Immediately there came to the hearers the inner witness of the Spirit that this was indeed "a word in season."

An example of this is given in Acts 15. There had been much argument among church leaders and members in Antioch and Jerusalem regarding the vexed question of circumcision for Gentile Christians. Among other speakers, Peter, Paul, and Barnabas had made their contribution to the great debate. Then arose the apostle James to utter that "word of wisdom" which found a glad "Amen" in the hearts of all who were present at the conference. They realized that the word of James on that occasion of special need was indeed from the Holy Ghost himself. Thus perfect agreement was reached and a very difficult problem solved (Acts 15:13–22, 28).

On the other hand, the "word of wisdom" can have a totally different effect upon some hardened sinners. This utterance of wisdom concerning the deep things of God so pierces their conscience that often they rail upon the God-sent messenger.

This was so in the case of Stephen, the Spirit-filled deacon. We read that the scoffers who listened to his message "were not able to resist the *wisdom* and the spirit by which he *spake*" (Acts 6:8–10). To Stephen, in that hour of crisis, was fulfilled the promise of

Jesus: "I will give you a *mouth* and *wisdom*, which all your adversaries shall not be able to gainsay or resist" (Luke 21:15).

Stephen's God-inspired word of wisdom cost him martyrdom.

The word of wisdom is given by the Holy Spirit, not for the lifting-up of men, but for the glory of God.

The word of knowledge

"To another the word of knowledge by the same Spirit" (I Cor. 12:8). This valuable gift, while related to intelligence and learning, is often bestowed upon Christians who have neither education nor acute practical judgment. For "the word of knowledge" referred to in I Corinthians 12:8 is not the product of a natural ability to explain, or analyze, or to follow to a logical conclusion.

This gift is given by the Holy Ghost alone, and can never be obtained by man's natural powers. This does not mean that the Lord ignores diligent and prayerful Bible study when He bestows the word of knowledge. Indeed, it will be found that the saint from whom comes this supernatural knowledge is usually both devout and disciplined. His piety and persevering meditation on the deep things of Scripture go hand-in-hand.

God encourages neither laziness nor false mysticism among His children. Nevertheless the fact remains that some saints, no matter how diligent in Bible study, will never possess that special word of knowledge which is the Spirit's prerogative to bestow.

To Peter the fisherman was given on several occasions the word of knowledge concerning the mysteries of Scripture. Although supernaturally bestowed, it went beyond the intuitive faculties of the heart in its appeal to the rational element in man.

Take, for example, the passage in II Peter 3:5–12.

In it the humble fisherman, under the inspiration of the Holy Ghost, gave a special word of knowledge concerning: (1) the principles underlying matter (vss. 5–7); (2) a great terminal wonder—the dissolution of this planet (vss. 10–12).

After the passing of 1900 years since Peter's remarkable utterance, present-day scientists marvel at the accurate knowledge of the apostle on matters which recently have been confirmed by nuclear research.

The gift of the word of knowledge seems basic in the office of the divinely appointed teacher in the church (I Cor. 12:28, 29). "It manifests the *Holy Spirit* operating through the teacher, and the intellectual powers at work are receiving their knowledge by a process of divine illumination. Such a teacher is truly a gift from Christ (Eph. 4:11), and one of the greatest blessings that can be bestowed upon the assemblies." [1]

In His infinite love and wisdom the Holy Spirit gives this special word of knowledge to selected saints in various denominational groups.

Coming to our own day, I think of at least four men (known to me personally) who, I believe, received this precious gift of the Holy Spirit. They are Harry E. Jessop (Church of the Nazarene), Donald Gee (Assemblies of God), Martin Lloyd-Jones (Congregational Church), and the late Samuel Chadwick (Methodist Church).

Oh that the Holy Spirit would give us many more teachers in the Church of Christ today! At this time of crisis we sorely need that "word of knowledge" which comes from heaven through sanctified human channels.

Discerning of spirits

"To another discerning of spirits" (I Cor. 12:10). The Church of Jesus Christ has always had to contend with the subtlety of Satan and evil spirits. Not only as a roaring lion, but also as an angel of light, does the prince of darkness seek to defeat the saints of the Most High. But the Holy Ghost has made abundant provision for the Church by arming her against the activities of demon powers. In the divine armory is the precious gift known as "discerning of spirits."

If ever the Church was in need of this spiritual gift it is surely today, when the very atmosphere of our towns and cities seems charged with satanic forces.

This gift of discernment must not be confused with that natural insight into human nature, which some people possess in a marked degree. The very name "discerning of *spirits*" seems to denote the ability to specially detect the nature of *spiritual* powers, rather than the purely natural activities of men. Of course, evil powers often work in and through human beings—hence the need of God-given ability to discern the subtle movings of Satan and demons behind what may appear to be of God. An outstanding example of this is found in Acts, chapter 16. There we read of a damsel possessed with an evil spirit of divination, who followed Paul and his colleagues for several days and cried: "These men are the servants of the Most High God, which shew unto us the way of salvation."

Paul discerned that it was not the Holy Spirit, but rather an evil spirit, who spoke through the girl. Therefore he commanded the demon to come out of her in the name of Jesus Christ (Acts 16:16–18).

Another striking instance of the value of the gift of discernment is recorded in Acts, chapter 8. Simon Magus had completely deceived even Philip the evangelist and had been baptized by him in the name of the Lord Jesus.

Now Philip would never have baptized anyone whom he thought was unsaved. That is clearly seen in his reply to the Ethiopian eunuch who wanted to be baptized in water. Said Philip: "If thou believest with all thine heart, thou mayest" (Acts 8:36, 37). Yet Philip failed to detect the hypocrisy of Simon Magus during the revival in Samaria. It was given to Peter, who possessed the gift of discerning spirits, to unmask the deception of the sorcerer and rebuke him publicly (Acts 8:13–23).

Thus the gift of discernment in the hands of a humble Spirit-filled believer is an offensive, as well as defensive, weapon against the kingdom of darkness. We stress the qualification, "a humble, Spirit-filled believer," because this wonderful gift of discernment calls for a right balance of humility and love in the person who possesses it.

Undoubtedly George Fox, the Quaker, and William Bramwell, the famous Methodist preacher, possessed the gift of discerning spirits. This proved of great value in their holy warfare against Satan. Both T. Bushel, a leading Ranter, and James Naylor, the Quaker, failed to deceive George Fox at a time when many were being led into error. In Bushel he saw "the nature of a beast" and rebuked him openly. "So I stopped his mouth, and all his fellow Ranters were silenced; for he was the head of them." [2]

As for poor James Naylor—the Friend whose error had deceived a number of other Quakers—there came to him the rebuke of George Fox in no uncertain manner. Fox, perceiving "there was now a wicked spirit risen up amongst Friends," refused the kiss that Naylor would have given him. Eventually Naylor repented of his sin, "and after some time he returned to truth again." [3]

In churches where prominence is given to the exercise of prophecy and the glossolalia (speaking in tongues), there is special need for the gift of discerning spirits to be in operation.

One Pentecostal leader has wisely stated: "Where supernatural manifestations appear, the gift of discernment will be a great safeguard ... so that should any possessed or actuated by evil spirits enter the church meeting and try to cause disorder or disturbance, the Spirit-filled leader will discern their satanic origin and take means to restrain them from manifesting their power. Instances could be cited where this has actually happened in the present day." [4]

The same writer has defined the gift of discernment as "the power given by the Holy Ghost to discern the spirit or spirits prompting an act or utterance. It is not just natural intuition, but a definite insight into these things given by the Holy Ghost." [5]

It was humble, Spirit-filled George Fox—the man of God who shook England in the 17th century—who testified: "The Lord had given me a spirit of discerning, by which I many times saw the states and conditions of people, and could try their spirits." [6]

---

[1] *Concerning Spiritual Gifts*, by Donald Gee, p. 25
[2] *The Journal of George Fox*: A Revised Text by Norman Penny, pp. 46–47
[3] *Ibid.*, p. 137
[4] *Spiritual Gifts in the Church*, by W. G. Hathaway, p. 39
[5] *Ibid.*, p. 38
[6] *The Journal of George Fox*, p. 85

CHAPTER FOURTEEN

The Gifts of the Spirit—
Prophecy, Tongues, and Interpretation

"TO ANOTHER PROPHECY; to another divers kinds of tongues; to another the interpretation of tongues" (I Cor. 12:10).

It cannot be denied that in past years there has been a strange mixture of the spiritual and the psychic in the exercise of the gifts of prophecy and tongues. On occasions there have been even demonic manifestations masquerading as divine operations.

Intelligent Pentecostal leaders admit this, and some, like the late George Jeffreys, have done their best to correct excesses in the modern Pentecostal Movement.

Some years ago, when conducting revival services in Barnsley, Yorkshire, I was confronted by a demon-possessed young man. From his lips there poured a torrent of words in an unknown tongue. In his frenzy the poor fellow clutched his face and began to throw off his clothes. Later he confessed to me that he had been dabbling in Spiritism. He said that at times a strange power would possess him, before which he was helpless. It was under this satanic influence that he spoke in tongues.

It is salutary to remember that the early days of the Apostolic Movement in Britain were sometimes sullied by false prophecies. Domestic tragedies resulted from obedience to certain utterances of the "prophets" in the local assembly. Nevertheless, the fact remains that there is a genuine gift of prophecy, as there is a Scriptural speaking in tongues and interpretation. To deny this is to hide our heads in the sands.

As Norman Grubb has said: "Tens of thousands of godly, Christ-loving people speak with tongues. Are they all deluded or fleshly or devil-possessed? I don't believe any fair investigator could say so." [1]

I have personally known gifted leaders like Donald Gee, Nelson Parr, George Jeffreys, Benjamin Griffiths and Randolph Murray. And I have met humble, saintly women who, like the above-mentioned brethren, have spoken in tongues. It may be that Dr. George E. Failing was right when he stated in his paper, "Developments in Holiness Theology after Wesley," "Pentecostalism is the protest movement of our day. It is a protest against the coldness of holiness denominations." [2]

The remarkable thing about the charismatic manifestations of the last two or three years is that, whereas until recently they were largely confined to that section of Christians we call Pentecostal, today the gift of tongues, along with the gift of healing, is operating in the older historic denominations.

The danger, as we see it, is the claim by many Pentecostals that speaking in tongues (even if only on one occasion) is the initial evidence of the baptism of the Spirit—and that only those who have thus spoken are filled with the Holy Ghost. This is divisive language and, apart from bringing doubt and confusion to many earnest believers, rules out multiplied thousands of saints whose lives and ministries were abundant proof of a Spirit-filled experience.

It has been my joy and privilege to know such giants in the Holy Ghost as Samuel Chadwick, David

Thomas, Paget Wilkes, John D. Drysdale, Rees How-
ells, Norman Grubb and Duncan Campbell. I have read
of John Wesley, Catherine Booth, Hugh Bourne, Evan
Roberts, Thomas Cook, Commissioner Samuel Brengle,
C. T. Studd and Billy Graham. There is no record that
any of these stalwarts spoke in other tongues. Yet what
person of spiritual perception would deny that they
were filled with the Holy Ghost?

And what of our blessed Saviour himself? There is
no mention of His speaking in tongues when anointed
with the Spirit at Jordan. Surely, if tongues is a "must"
as evidence of the Spirit's baptism, it would have been
recorded that Jesus had this manifestation!

We are glad that certain Pentecostal leaders have
had both discernment and courage to acknowledge that
a person can be filled with the Holy Spirit without
speaking in tongues. Among them were the late T. B.
Barratt and George Jeffreys. Even more authoritative
is the statement by the European Pentecostal Conference held in Stockholm in the early summer of 1939. It
admitted that tongues might occur *apart* from the
Spirit's action; and that a Christian could be filled
with the Spirit without the sign of tongues.

In May 1963 there appeared in the *Alliance Weekly*
an official statement by the Board of Managers of
The Christian and Missionary Alliance which was
most timely. It was entitled: "Where We Stand on the
Revived Tongues Movement," and was the judgment
of the Society after over 50 years' experience on the
subject of the gifts of the Holy Spirit.

The Board of Managers declared: "What may appear new to some groups is not new to the Alliance.
We still have scars to show for our battle for truth
from the days when we stood against some who denied
the gifts of the Spirit and others who insisted that
tongues was the evidence of the baptism of the Spirit."

Some 56 years ago Dr. A. B. Simpson, founder of the Christian and Missionary Alliance, made a study of the charismatic movement which was then sweeping the United States and which affected members of the Alliance. His findings were reported to the General Council and adopted by them as the official position of the Society.

After over half a century the position of the Alliance is unaltered regarding the glossolalia. It endorses the Annual Report for the year 1907–1908, which stated: "We believe there can be no doubt that in many cases remarkable outpourings of the Holy Spirit have been accompanied with genuine instances of the gift of tongues and many extraordinary manifestations. Many of these experiences appear not only to be genuine but accompanied by a spirit of deep humility, earnestness and soberness, and free from extravagance and error. . . . It would, therefore, be a very serious matter for any candid Christian to pass a wholesale criticism or condemnation upon such movements or presume to limit the Holy One of Israel.

"But at the same time . . . there are other developments which make it very plain that those who have been made shepherds of the flocks of God and stewards of the mysteries of Christ have need to guard with firm and fearless hand God's truth and work, seeking from Him the spirit of 'discernment concerning things that differ' and carefully guarding the little flock from seducing spirits and false teachers.

"One of these greatest errors is a disposition to make special manifestations an evidence of the baptism of the Holy Ghost, giving to them the name of Pentecost, as though none had received the Spirit of Pentecost but those who had the power to speak in tongues, thus leading many sincere Christians to cast away their confidence, plunging them in perplexity and darkness or causing them to seek after special manifestations of other than God himself. Another grave tendency is the disposition to turn aside from the great trust which God has given us in the salvation of sinners and the sanctification of believers, and seek for signs and wonders and special manifestations."

The Board of Managers added: "The present revival of interest in spiritual gifts is such that it cannot be ignored. We must deal with it as becomes dedicated Christians, in full charity and with cordial understanding. Certainly some persons of impeccable Christian character are associated with the present charismatic movement. But the gift of tongues belongs in the category of things easily imitated and by the very nature of it is capable of abuses and wild excesses. . . .

"We believe the Scriptural teaching to be that the gift of tongues is one of the gifts of the Spirit, and that it may be present in the normal Christian assembly as a sovereign bestowal of the Holy Spirit upon such as He wills. We do not believe that all Christians should possess the gift of tongues. The gift is one of many gifts and is given to some for the benefit of all. The attitude toward the gift of tongues held by pastor and people should be: 'Seek not, forbid not.' This we hold to be part of wisdom for this hour."

The gift of prophecy mentioned in I Corinthians 12:10 evidently refers to a certain degree of inspired utterance which is profitable for "edification, and exhortation, and comfort." The person possessing this spiritual gift is "greater than he that speaketh with tongues, except he interpret" (I Cor. 14:5).

Prophecy

This gift of prophecy seems to have been in common use in the early church. Paul told the Corinthians

that *all* could prophesy one by one in the assembly
(I Cor. 14:31). A distinction must be made, however,
between those ordinary church members who possessed the gift of prophecy and that clearly defined
class who were officially regarded as prophets. Judas,
Silas, and Agabus were in that class (Acts 15:32; 21:
10). They definitely foretold certain coming events.

In more modern times we have had striking examples of official prophets in the Church in the persons
of George Fox, Alexander Peden and John Welch. Some
of their prophecies were startling but sure.

A word of caution is needed here. As Donald Gee
has wisely pointed out: "Even in an official sense, the
New Testament prophet occupies a very different place
from the great prophets of the Old Testament. Samuel,
for instance (I Sam. 3:20), was the recognized spokes-
man not only for Jehovah to the people but for the
people to Jehovah (ch. 8:21).

"All this is changed in the New Testament dispensation ushered in at Pentecost. It is now the privilege
of *all* believers to be personally led by the Spirit of
God (Rom. 8:14).

"It cannot be too emphatically stated that we need
neither prophet nor priest to come between ourselves
and the Lord in this present dispensation; and to submit for one moment to such a system is a definite
step backwards into bondage." [3]

The tragedy of noble Edward Irving is a warning
to all those who would implicitly rely upon "prophetic"
utterance for guidance.

Although the spiritual gift of prophecy is an inspired utterance which includes "forthtelling" as well
as "foretelling," it is something different from ordinary
preaching.

In the exercise of the gift of prophecy the utterance
is more from the impulse of a sudden revelation or in-

spiration than from a carefully prepared discourse. The idea of speaking from an immediate revelation (Greek: *apokalupsis*) seems clear from the words of I Corinthians 14:29, 30: "Let the prophets speak two or three, and another judge. If anything be *revealed* to another that sitteth by, let the first hold his peace."

Repeatedly it must be emphasized that this extraordinary and valuable gift of prophecy (which, says Paul, we are to covet) must be rightly guarded and controlled by the infallible *written* word of Scripture. Only then is it a means of spiritual edification and comfort to the saints.

Tongues and Interpretation

The mysterious glossolalia of I Corinthians 12 and 14 seems to be quite different from the speaking in tongues on the Day of Pentecost. At Pentecost definite languages of earth were miraculously spoken by the Spirit-filled disciples. There was no need of an interpreter. The Upper Room phenomenon led immediately to the salvation of 3,000 sinners who heard the disciples "speak in our tongues the wonderful works of God."

It is an undisputed fact that the late Rev. Walter Searle, the well-known preacher and missionary (one-time secretary of the South African General Mission), was so wrought upon by the Holy Ghost while preaching one day to the natives through an interpreter that suddenly he began to preach fluently in the African language he had not learned. This miracle continued for at least three months and caused a great stir among the natives.

But when we come to the Corinthian church charismatic manifestations, we have a mystery that calls for very careful investigation. Paul distinctly said that "he that speaketh in an unknown tongue speaketh not unto men, but unto God: for no man understandeth him; howbeit in the spirit he speaketh mysteries" (I Cor. 14:2). The apostle lays it down that this mysterious gift is not to be exercised in the gathering of the saints unless there is an "interpreter" present. Even then not more than three utterances are allowed in one meeting (I Cor. 14:27, 28).

The wise pastor will take care to prevent fleshly and demonic utterances in the assembly (how needful is the gift of the "discerning of spirits" when charismatic manifestations are in operation!). He will insist that those who want to exercise tongues and interpretations are not casual visitors of doubtful reputation, but are tried and respected members of the local assembly.

Although Paul himself thanked God that he spoke with tongues more than all the Corinthian believers, yet he confessed: "In the church I had rather speak five words with my understanding, that by my voice I might teach others also, than ten thousand words in an unknown tongue."

It was the carnal state of the Corinthians that caused them to use the precious gifts of the Holy Spirit as children use their toys in the nursery. The gift of tongues was used almost as a "rattle" to make as much noise and confusion as possible! It is only the truly sanctified, Spirit-filled Christians who know how to exercise in meekness the gifts of the Holy Ghost. Walking in the more excellent way of perfect love, they do not "show off" in the assembly, but ever seek to edify their fellow Christians and to glorify God. They follow closely the admonition of the Spirit himself: "Let everything be done decently and in order."

---

1 *God Unlimited*, p. 69
2 *Insights into Holiness*, p. 31
3 *Concerning Spiritual Gifts*, p. 43

CHAPTER FIFTEEN

The Pentecost of Romans

"THE PENTECOST OF ROMANS" is an apt title for the eighth chapter of that wonderful epistle. It stands out in marked contrast to the seventh chapter, in which the Holy Spirit is not mentioned once. But in the eighth chapter the Holy Spirit is referred to not less than 19 times. Therein lies the secret of the amazing difference between Romans seven and eight.

In chapter seven is stark tragedy. It is the portrait of a man at war with himself. He fights the worst of all conflicts, that of *civil war*. He is divided, defeated, and in despair. Although deeply religious he has a "split" personality. Listen to his confession: "I delight in the law of God after the inward man: but I see another law in my members, warring against the law of my mind" (Rom. 7:22, 23).

Such a civil war ends in abject defeat. So Paul cries out, bringing me into captivity to the law of sin which is in my members . . . for the good that I would I do not: but the evil which I would not, that I do. I am carnal, sold under sin" (Rom. 7:14, 19, 23).

Such defeat leads to despair. The defeated warrior wails: "O wretched man that I am."

Man cannot be happy while he is a slave to sin;

God made him to be a king, a conqueror, a glad soldier. Man can never rest satisfied until he has found the secret of victory over sin.

During one of my visits to South Africa I listened to the striking testimony of an influential Christian farmer. He told me of that sad period in his life when, in spite of all his efforts to live a victorious Christian life, he repeatedly sank into grievous failure. His besetting sins were tobacco and a vile temper. So vicious was his temper that native Africans did not want to work for him. Although badly needing employment, they were most reluctant to serve this professing Christian farmer.

Mr. K—— confessed to me that at times his despair was so great that he contemplated suicide. More than once he took his gun to shoot himself, but every time he did so he was restrained by a voice which clearly said, "Eternity."

Then one glorious day there came a complete transformation to this farmer. While praying alone and reading God's Word (it was the promise of Jesus in Luke 11:13), he entered by faith into Romans, chapter eight! The spiritual revolution in his life was so remarkable that the natives for miles around radically changed in their attitude to him. Now they sensed the love of God in his heart towards them, and eagerly sought employment on his farm. Instead of anger in his heart for the natives, Mr. K—— sought to win them for Jesus Christ. Through his sanctified efforts a mission station was raised up. Today it is the North Carolina Mission Center of the Church of the Nazarene!

If chapter seven of Romans is one of stark tragedy, chapter eight is one of scintillating triumph. Again there is the picture of a man fighting a fierce battle, with tremendous odds against him. But he is not engaged in a civil war; rather does he fight in a foreign assignment against an enemy from outside. And he emerges more than conqueror. Defeat has changed to victory's ringing cheer. Why? Because of the incoming of the Holy Ghost to fully possess a consecrated disciple of Jesus Christ.

Exulting in the manifold benefits of the Spirit-filled life, Paul exclaims:

I have freedom. "The law of the Spirit of life in Christ Jesus hath made me free from the law of sin and death" (vs. 2).

I have guidance. "For as many as are *led* by the Spirit of God, they are the sons of God" (vs. 14).

I have assurance. "The Spirit himself beareth witness with our spirit that we are the children of God" (vs. 16).

I have power in prayer. "Likewise the Spirit helpeth our infirmities: for we know not what we should pray for as we ought: but the Spirit himself maketh intercession for us with groanings which cannot be uttered" (vs. 26).

I have a glorious future. "For I reckon that the sufferings of this present time are not worthy to be compared with the glory which shall be revealed in us" (vs. 18).

I have supernatural victory in all the circumstances of life. "In all these things we are more than conquerors" (vs. 37).

Paul describes the sphere, the quality, and the secret of this abounding victory.

Its sphere. In "tribulation, distress, persecution, famine, nakedness, peril and sword" (vs. 35).

In all these areas of testing, the Spirit-filled Christian is more than conqueror.

Its quality. "More than conquerors." I once heard my friend Kenneth Bedwell (a noted missionary in Africa) say that the Zulu rendering of the phrase "more than conquerors" is "victory over victory." The story is told of a rather pompous Bible-class teacher who, thinking to expose the ignorance of a humble member of his group, asked the question: "What is meant by the words 'more than conqueror'?"

After a moment's thought the old saint replied: "It means that you fight 12 men and kill 13!" Crude, maybe, but effective.

Its secret. "Through him that loved us" (vs. 37).

Christ has purchased complete victory for us at Calvary. There He "spoiled principalities and powers: made a show of them openly, triumphing over them in himself" (Col. 2:15).

On the cross Jesus not only bare our sins that we might be pardoned; He also took there our "old man," that "the body of sin might be destroyed, that henceforth we should not serve sin" (Rom. 6:6).

But that victory is ours only when the Holy Spirit does *in* us what Jesus did *for* us at Calvary. Because of His perfect work on the cross Jesus was exalted to the right hand of God's throne; having received of the Father the promise of the Holy Ghost, He has now shed Him forth abundantly (Acts 2:23).

Only through the indwelling Holy Spirit can we enjoy this life of abounding victory. It is something to be *received*, and not *achieved*. We can never live this life of victory by *imitation*: it comes only by *indwelling*.

Let the weary, defeated soul come now to the Christ who purchased the victory and who alone can fill with the Holy Ghost. Let him ask just now, with an obedient, trusting heart. The Lord will answer immediately.

While campaigning recently in a northwest American city, a fine young preacher came to see me. He was the minister of a community church and had labored hard to win souls for Christ. Conscious of frustration and wrong tempers, he longed for an experience of perfect love, of victory in the Holy Ghost.

His opening remark to me was significant. "I want," said he, "to graduate from Romans seven to Romans eight."

Then he told me of his search for entire sanctification. He had read books on the subject and had prayed fervently for a life of constant victory. But this pearl of greatest price had eluded him.

It was evident to me that this earnest young man was fully consecrated to God. He had obeyed the apostolic injunction in Romans 12:1, 2, "I beseech you therefore, brethren, by the mercies of God, that ye present your bodies a living sacrifice . . . and be not conformed to this world."

But he was still outside the blessing of Romans eight. Consecration in itself had not brought the coveted gift of purity and power. What this young minister now needed was appropriating faith in the promises of God. So I not only read to him the glorious words of Romans 6:6 and I Thessalonians 5:23, 24, I also pointed him to Galatians 3:14, Acts 15:8, 9, and Acts 26:18:

"That we might receive the promise of the Spirit through faith."

"Giving them the Holy Ghost . . . purifying their hearts by faith."

"Sanctified by faith that is in me."

I endeavored to show him that it is by simple faith in the faithfulness of God that we enter into the experience of Romans eight.

The young minister saw the truth, then dropped on his knees and with childlike simplicity claimed his inheritance in Christ. He arose with the glad assurance of victory in the Holy Ghost.

He had graduated from Romans seven to Romans eight!

CHAPTER SIXTEEN

Recovering the Lost Glory

1. *The Former Glory*

THE ACTS 2 PENTECOST ushered in the most privileged dispensation known to man since his expulsion from Eden. It seems evident that, before the Fall, Adam possessed not only the principle of natural life but also the grace and indwelling of the Holy Spirit. Genesis, chapter 2, tells us that God breathed into a temple of clay the breath of life and man became a living soul. He was God's masterpiece, made in the moral and intellectual likeness of his Creator.

To unfallen Adam was given a glory far greater than we can imagine. It was the glory of holiness and dominion. In his radiant purity man enjoyed not only unclouded fellowship with God but also kingship over the earth. The great promise to Adam was: "Have dominion over the fish of the sea, and over the fowl of the air . . . and over every living thing that creepeth upon the earth."

The eighth psalm, which is an expansion of that ancient promise, is a magnificent lyric on the glory of man as God intended it to be. In verses five and six of that psalm the Authorized Version reads: "For thou hast made him a little lower than the angels, and hast crowned him with glory and honour. Thou madest him to have dominion over the works of thy hands."

These words are a correct translation of the Greek of that psalm, but they do not correctly translate the original Hebrew in which it was written. In the original Hebrew it was stated that man was made a little lower than the *Elohim*. Now *Elohim* is the regular Hebrew word for God. So what the Psalmist actually wrote concerning unfallen man was: "For thou hast made him a little less than God." This in fact is the translation of the American Revised Standard Version of the eighth psalm. The French Bible also renders it in this way.

2. *The Fatal Fall*

The tragic fall in Eden did not take from Adam the principle of natural life, for he lived another nine hundred years on this earth. But it robbed him of the priceless grace and indwelling of the Holy Spirit. Thus Adam lost his holiness and dominion. As a result man is now only a pale shadow of what God intended him to be. He who should be free is fettered; he who should be monarch is a slave.

How right G. K. Chesterton was when he said that "whatever else is or is not true, this one thing is certain: man is not what he was meant to be."

Down the ages that followed Adam's expulsion from Eden, man often cried out for his lost inheritance. Meant for the heights, made for sovereignty, fallen man felt he could not fulfill his destiny without power. But he miserably failed in his efforts to achieve spiritual dominion. Ovid, the greatest poet of the Augustan cycle, confessed:

"My reason this: my passion that persuades;
 I see the right, and I approve it too,
 Condemn the wrong, and yet the wrong pursue."

A greater than Ovid, even the Apostle Paul, when writing of his unconverted state, exclaimed: "For I delight in the law of God after the inward man: but I see another law in my members, warring against the law of my mind, and bringing me into captivity to the law of sin which is in my members. O wretched man that I am! who shall deliver me?"

Only One could restore to man what he had lost through Adam's transgression. He was the blessed Holy Spirit. He had brooded over primeval darkness and chaos, and had brought forth cosmos and light. But He had sadly withdrawn His presence from the human heart and had left it ruined and desolate.

3. The Promise of Recovery

Promises of the return of the Holy Spirit to man had been given by God in Old Testament days. Through such prophets as Isaiah, Ezekiel, and Joel, the word of the Lord came concerning the Holy Spirit.

In chapter 44 of his prophecy, Isaiah wrote: "Thus saith the Lord that made thee: ... I will pour my Spirit upon thy seed, and my blessing upon thine offspring."

In Ezekiel, chapter 36, the promise was more explicit. It declared: "Thus saith the Lord God: ... a new heart also will I give you, and a new spirit will I put within you. ... And I will put my Spirit within you, and cause you to walk in my statutes."

It was, however, the great promise in Joel's prophecy which was applied by Peter to the outpouring of the Holy Spirit on the Day of Pentecost. "This is that which was spoken by the prophet Joel," cried the apostle to the Jerusalem multitudes.

When Christ came He confirmed and clarified the Old Testament promises concerning the Holy Spirit.

He brought them into shining focus by declaring that
the "promise of the Father" meant the coming of a
divine Person to indwell and empower His disciples.
During that memorable after-supper talk in the Pass-
over room, Jesus said that "He [the Holy Spirit] shall
be *in you*."

Just over forty days later there came the breath-
taking promise of the risen Lord: "Ye shall be baptized
with the Holy Ghost not many days hence."

What a thrilling moment it must have been! At
long last, after the weary waiting of the ages, man was
to become again, in a sense unknown since the fall of
Adam, the temple of the Holy Spirit.

What made such a miracle possible? It was the
glorious work which the resurrected Christ had accom-
plished. Just as John the Baptist had prepared the way
for Christ's first coming, so Jesus prepared the way for
the advent of the Holy Spirit.

In which way had He done this? First by His teaching and then by His atonement. Sin had to be effectively
dealt with before the Holy Spirit could again take up
His abode in the human heart. It was sin that had driven
Him away from the first Adam. So until Jesus Christ
had died on the cross and had risen again from the dead,
thus "putting away sin by the sacrifice of himself," the
promise of the Father could not be realized. ("The Holy
Ghost was not yet given; because that Jesus was not
yet glorified."—John 7:39)

So it was the risen and triumphant Christ—He who
had made full atonement for sin—who declared to His
disciples: "Ye shall be baptized with the Holy Ghost
not many days hence."

4. *The Purpose of the Promise*

Even after the Resurrection, the apostles had a

wrong conception of what it meant to be filled with the Holy Spirit. Hence their question: "Wilt thou at this time restore again the kingdom of Israel?" They associated the coming of the Holy Spirit with the bestowment of temporal power, with the immediate restoration of Israel's former glory.

In reply Jesus did not say that the kingdom—with all its splendor—would not be restored to Israel. But He revealed the true and immediate purpose for which the Father would send the Holy Ghost. He said: "*Ye shall receive power*, after that the Holy Ghost is come upon you; and ye shall be witnesses unto me."

Notice that the Greek word translated "power" in verse eight of Acts, chapter one, is a different one from that used in verse seven. The word in verse seven is *exousia*, which means "authority," but the word in our text is *dunamis*, which signifies "ability." Now there is a difference between *authority* and *ability*, between *right* and *efficiency*.

Even before Pentecost the apostles were given the right or the authority to represent their Master and His kingdom. They were truly converted men, for their names were written in heaven, and they were "not of this world," even as Christ was not of this world (Luke 10:20 and John 17:14). But although they possessed authority as Christ's apostles, they did not possess the ability (*dunamis*) to fully exercise their right.

Time and again they miserably failed in the hour of testing. Jesus made it clear that the baptism of the Holy Spirit would give His weak and defeated followers the power they needed to be His witnesses even unto the ends of the earth. In other words, they were to become effective representatives of their risen Lord. The Holy Spirit effected this miracle by making them Christ-

like in character and ministry. They were made pure
and powerful.

There could be no genuine baptism of the Spirit
apart from *a thorough purging of their hearts from all
carnality*. So the emblem of the Spirit on the Day of
Pentecost was not the gentle dove but a cloven tongue
of fire—the symbol of *dynamic purification*.

Samuel Chadwick has well said: "The sign of a
Christian Church is not a crucifix, but fire . . . the token
of the divine presence is the fire of the Holy Ghost.
When we pray for a baptism of the Holy Ghost, we are
praying that God will send through our nature this
searching, scorching flame, that it may burn up in
heart and life whatever is earthly and sinful."

It is significant that the adjective "holy" is used of
the Spirit of God over ninety times in the Bible. It is
His special office to make men holy.

But the promised Comforter not only purged the
hearts of the waiting disciples in the Upper Room; He
also filled them with His own glorious presence. "They
were all filled with the Holy Ghost." It was His indwelling fulness that made them like their risen Lord;
the Holy Spirit has been aptly called "Christ's other
self."

A study of the Acts of the Apostles reveals the regal
way in which Spirit-filled Christians represented their
Master. Within thirty years of the Day of Pentecost
the gospel had spread from Palestine to Syria, through
nearly all the numerous districts of Asia Minor, through
Greece and the islands of the Aegean Sea, the coast of
Africa, and Rome itself.

Dominion had come to powerless disciples, and they
exercised a kingliness which caused men to call them
"Christians" or "Christ's men." Their contemporaries
could truly say of them.

"Everywhere with shoutings loud,
    Shouts that shake the gates of hell,
Thy anointed witness-cloud
    Of Thy great redemption tell."

Theirs was not the carnal sovereignty which is grasped by worldly men. It was not the power of self-assertion in the quest for self-realization. It was the *dunamis* which flowed from Christ-centered, Spirit-filled men and women. Christ when on earth had revealed the nature of His heavenly Father to men. So now His Spirit-baptized followers showed forth the nature of the risen Christ to a sinful world. They *reflected* His *radiance*, His *humility*, and His *fathomless love*.

The risen Christ is no longer the "Man of Sorrows." He has been anointed with the oil of gladness above His fellows. He is the Lord of glory, the Radiant One at the Father's right hand. After Pentecost His disciples became radiant Christians. In fact, when Stephen, the Spirit-filled deacon, was about to be martyred, his accusers "saw his face as it had been the face of an angel."

The late Dr. G. Campbell Morgan told of a girl who was walking up and down the platform of a railway station, waiting for a train. In her heart was the blessed Holy Spirit. As she walked the platform her face became transformed with the joy of the Lord. In a first-class carriage sat a lady of title, wealth, and culture. She saw the girl pass several times in front of the train, called to her, and asked: "What makes you look so happy?"

The girl told her simple story, and the result of that brief conversation was that the titled lady was led to the same Christ.

Dr. Morgan said: "I knew both women, and can testify to the truth of the incident."

A sorrowing world badly needs the sight of a radiant church. Only the indwelling Spirit can give the radiance.

Furthermore, the risen Christ is still clothed with meekness. We read in John's Gospel, chapter 21, that He appeared to His discouraged disciples on the Sea of Tiberias and invited them to partake of a meal which He had prepared.

The resurrected Lord was still eager to serve His weary followers. After Pentecost that same *humility* was evident in the lives of those disciples who, before they were Spirit-filled, had quarrelled among themselves as to who should be the greatest. Peter became so humble that even when thrilled by the miracle he had wrought upon the cripple at the Beautiful Gate of the Temple, he could say to his admirers, "Why look ye so earnestly on us . . . ? His name hath made this man strong."

Philip, the gifted evangelist, was so possessed by the Holy Ghost that he was far more concerned about representing his risen Saviour than in preaching so many sermons before admiring crowds. So he willingly consented to serve tables during the crisis which arose in the Jerusalem church.

The power of the Holy Spirit does not make us like strutting peacocks or towering giraffes, but it enables us to show forth the humility of the Christ who dwells in our hearts by faith. The fruit of the Spirit is meekness.

Finally, let us never forget that the Pentecostal baptism also gives ability to Christians to reveal the *boundless love* of Christ to a needy, hate-ridden world. Paul tells us that the love of God is shed abroad in our hearts by the Holy Ghost (Rom. 5:5). It was the Spirit-filled Stephen who, possessed with compassion for his enemies, cried out in his dying agony, "Lord, lay not this sin to their charge." He died a conqueror on the battlefield, and the trumpets sounded for him on the other side.

Thomas Cook, the famous Methodist evangelist and college principal, used to tell of a young man whom he once met in the waiting room of a Leeds railway station. The young man sat weeping, with his head buried in his hands. When asked if he was in trouble, he replied, "I am not in trouble now, but I never expected to meet any man who would do for me what I believed Jesus Christ would do." Then he told his story.

He and his brother had opened an engineering business and had bought a gas engine from the well-known firm of Frank Crossley in Manchester, England. Unfortunately the engine was too small for the work required, and so the business declined and the two brothers were faced with ruin.

The young man had gone to Manchester to see if he could remedy the situation but was told by the manager of the Crossley firm that, seeing he had received the very type of engine ordered, nothing more could be done unless the brothers bought a larger one. This they could not do.

Just then Frank Crossley came on the scene and listened patiently to the young man's pathetic story. Taking him into his office, Frank Crossley said: "Go back and tell your brother that I will install a larger gas engine, and it will not cost you a penny extra. Also ask him to let me know how much money you have lost in your business since buying my gas engine, and I will send you a check to cover that amount."

Thomas Cook was delighted to tell the young man that Frank Crossley was a personal friend of his.

The Christian world knows that Frank Crossley was not only a successful business magnate; it knows also that he left his mansion in the country and went to live among the poor people in Ancoats, Manchester. There he built the well-known Star Hall for the proclamation of Scriptural holiness. It was in Star Hall that wonderful conventions were held, conventions which drew to its platform some of the finest holiness preachers in the world.

Frank Crossley taught and experienced the baptism of the Holy Spirit as a second, definite work of grace in the Christian's life. To him it gave the ability to reveal to many people, including the young engineer, the boundless compassion of Christ. It was a power that broke through the hard crust of indifference and cynicism. No wonder that 16,000 people came to Frank Crossley's funeral!

> Love ever gives—forgives—outlives,
> And ever stands with open hands;
> And while it lives, it gives.
> For this is love's prerogative—
> To give—and give—and give.

In the closing days of this dispensation God is waiting to give His people another Pentecost. To meet the soon returning King of Glory, and to reveal His grace and power to a lost world, the church needs to be *filled* with the Holy Spirit. Then, and not till then, will she go forth "as fair as the moon, clear as the sun, and terrible as an army with banners."

There are three simple conditions for being filled with the Holy Spirit. They are made crystal clear in the New Testament. They are these:

First, *ask*. "How much more shall your heavenly Father give the Holy Spirit to them that *ask* him?" (Luke 11:13).

Second, *obey*. "The Holy Ghost, whom God hath

given to them that *obey* him" (Acts 5:32).

Third, *believe*. "That we might receive the promise of the Spirit through faith" (Gal. 3:14).

> God's skies are full of Pentecosts,
>   For you, for me, for all;
> Then let us humbly, boldly press,
> Our heritage in Christ possess,
>   That power from heaven may fall.
>   Amen

CHAPTER SEVENTEEN

The Spirit Speaks to the Churches

THE RISEN LORD JESUS SPEAKS to His Church on earth by the Holy Spirit. This is clearly seen in the Book of the Revelation, where repeatedly the message of Christ to His saints is immediately followed by the words: "He that hath an ear to hear, let him hear what the Spirit saith unto the churches" (Rev. 3:6, 13, 22).

Out of the many Christian assemblies in Asia Minor in the days of the apostle John, only seven are mentioned in the Revelation.

This is because they are representative of the Church of Jesus on earth not only at that time, but also throughout the Christian dispensation. For seven in Scripture is the number of completion.

It is very significant that only two out of the seven Asian churches escape censure from Christ. The other five are rebuked and called upon to repent. This state of things is true also of the Church of Jesus today—right on the eve of His second advent.

It would seem that only a minority of the Lord's people on earth fully satisfy His loving heart.

The two assemblies without blame in the Revelation are Smyrna and Philadelphia. Their names reveal their character.

Thus "Smyrna" means "myrrh," a fragrant perfume or spice, highly prized by the ancient Hebrews. It was an ingredient in the holy anointing oil used in the consecration of the priests of Israel and in the dedication of the Tabernacle (Ex. 30:22–30).

The characteristic tear-like drops of gum resin which exuded from the myrrh tree flowed more copiously when the tree was wounded. This speaks of a fragrance which is brought out more freely under suffering and trial. This was so with the church at Smyrna. It was outwardly poor and was called to endure much testing: "The devil shall cast some of you into prison, that ye may be tried; and ye shall have tribulation ten days." But in Christ's eyes this sorely tested church was fragrant and wealthy. Hence His verdict: "Thou art rich" (Rev. 2:9).

How different was the Master's judgment upon the self-satisfied Laodiceans. "Thou knowest not that thou art poor" (ch. 3:17).

It is the saints who patiently and meekly suffer for Christ who are the most fruitful. They are exceedingly precious in His sight.

> Wherever you ripe fields behold,
> Waving to God their sheaves of gold,
> Be sure, some corn of wheat has died,
> Some soul has there been crucified;
> Someone has wrestled, wept and prayed,
> And fought hell's legions undismayed:
> There is no gain without a loss.
> You cannot save but by a cross.

The name "Philadelphia" means "brotherly love." In connection with the Asian assembly it evidently pointed to its large-heartedness. It was a church of the "open door"—patient, faithful and missionary-hearted.

Thus Christ could say to this group: "Thou hast kept the word of my patience, and hast not denied my name. I have set before thee an open door, and no man can shut it."

It is no wonder that the Philadelphia Church endured so long. A fact of history is that Philadelphia was the last Christian city that submitted to the Turks. Of the seven cities mentioned in these addresses, it had the longest duration. It is the only one whose name has been preserved to modern times. Even today it is remembered by the well-known American city founded by William Penn the Quaker.

How true it is that self-centeredness and ultra-denominationalism spell decay and defeat to any single Christian or to any religious group. What a revealing word is Paul's concerning Timothy, his son in the gospel! He says to the Philippian church: "I have no man so dear unto me, who will naturally care for your estate. *For all seek their own*, not the things which are Jesus Christ's" (Phil. 2:20, 21).

The truly missionary-hearted spirit—which is the hall mark of a Pentecostal experience—"seeketh not her own," but longs for the advancement of Christ's kingdom everywhere. We cannot gainsay the fact that God is specially blessing in these end-time days evangelical inter-denominational efforts to win the "outsiders" for Christ.

The example of Philadelphia should be a warning against mere sectarianism and an encouragement to real catholicity.

When we come to the other five churches mentioned in the Revelation, we naturally ask the question, "What was wrong with them? Why did they fail to satisfy the Master? Their names are: Ephesus, Pergamos, Thyatira, Sardis and Laodicea.

Their defects may be summed up in this way:

1. *With Ephesus it was lack of love.* "Thou hast left thy first love" (Rev. 2:4).

The Holy Spirit here unveils the risen Lord as the ardent Lover who will not be satisfied with anything less than our white-hot devotion for himself. Outwardly all was well with the Ephesian church. Even an archangel might not have detected anything wrong. In fact, Christ himself pays them this tribute: "Thou canst not bear them which are evil; and hast tried them which say they are apostles, and are not and hast found them liars: And hast borne, and hast laboured, and hast not fainted" (ch. 2:2, 3).

What gigantic virtues! What quenchless zeal! What shining qualities of character! Here are orthodoxy, discernment, endurance, patience and sacrificial service. And yet all these in themselves fail to satisfy the heart of Jesus. So He cries out, "I have somewhat against thee, because thou hast left thy first love" (ch. 2:4). Nothing but a personal, flaming devotion for himself can satiate His holy passion.

It is sadly possible for the good to become the enemy of the best. The very activities of Christian service can sometimes crowd out the Christ; and the gifts of the Spirit, valuable though they are, can, unless permeated with love, obscure the vision of the great Giver of the gifts—the Holy Ghost himself.

Martha of Bethany served in the presence of Jesus. But her spirit, although sacrificial, lacked that vital element which could make her service well-pleasing to the Master.

We read that she was "cumbered about much serving" (Luke 10:40). The Greek word here translated "cumbered" could be rendered "distracted." Martha was distraught by a multiplicity of duties.

As J. B. Phillips has rendered it: "Martha was very worried about her elaborate preparations." In spite of her culinary skill she misjudged the tastes of her distinguished Guest! She lacked that true spirit of worship which is the secret of pleasing Jesus. Mary, however, with the intuitive power of love went straight to the root of effective Christian service.

She sat at Jesus' feet and heard His word. Her supreme joy was to hear the music of His voice. So delighted was Christ with Mary's choice that He passed a verdict which has echoed down the centuries: "One thing is needful: and Mary hath chosen that good part, which shall not be taken away from her."

2. *With Pergamos the trouble was lack of sound doctrine.* "Thou hast there them that hold the doctrine of Balaam, who taught Balac to cast a stumbling block before the children of Israel. So hast thou also them that hold the doctrine of the Nicolaitans, which thing I hate" (Rev. 2:14–16).

The lesson to be learned from Christ's rebuke to the Pergamos church is that it *does* matter what we believe. We must be sound in doctrine. It is nonsense to say that so long as a person is sincere it doesn't matter what he believes. What a fallacy this is!

Dr. Stanley Jones tells of three Hindus who cut out their tongues and offered them to Kali, one of the Hindu goddesses. There was a time in India when mothers threw their choicest babies into the river Ganges in order to satisfy the gods.

Thus, because of false doctrine, sincere people mutilated their bodies and slew their precious children!

There is always a vital connection between sound doctrine and holy living. Paul realized this vital truth, so he emphasized it repeatedly in his epistles to Timothy and Titus.

To Timothy he said, "I besought thee to abide still at Ephesus . . . that thou mightest charge some that they teach no other doctrine." "Give attendance to reading . . . to doctrine . . . . Take heed unto thyself, and unto the doctrine" (I Tim. 1:3; 4:13, 16).

To Titus Paul wrote, "Speak thou the things which become sound doctrine" (Tit. 2:3).

Let us not forget that Jesus *hated* the doctrine of the Nicolaitans. John, the apostle of love, also warned Christians against purveyors of false doctrine. In fact he commanded them to forbid such people entrance into their homes and to refrain from wishing them God speed (II John 9:10).

"Harsh words," did you say? Remember they came from the burning heart of one who, five times over in the Gospel of John, is called the disciple whom Jesus loved!

In view of the clear warnings of the Holy Ghost, how vital is careful Bible study in these days of loose doctrine. It is imperative that we study to show ourselves approved unto God, workmen "who need not to be ashamed, rightly dividing the word of truth" (II Tim. 2:15).

If we read three-and-a-third chapters of the Bible daily, we would read through the whole Book in twelve months. But how many Christians have read the Scriptures right through even once? No wonder the modern professing Christian is such an easy prey to the false doctrines so persuasively peddled from door to door by zealous Mormons, Jehovah's Witnesses, and the like.

True revival will never come until there is first a return to devout and diligent reading of the Scriptures and an implicit faith in their authority.

3. *The church at Thyatira lacked moral purity.* "I have somewhat against thee, because thou sufferest that woman Jezebel . . . to teach and seduce my servants to commit fornication, and to eat things sacrificed unto idols" (Rev. 2:20).

Lack of fervent love for Christ leads to lack of sound doctrine; lack of sound doctrine often leads to wrong conduct. The experience of entire sanctification does not destroy our purely human nature with its legitimate instincts and appetites. It is the carnal mind, that infection of nature inherited from Adam, which is cleansed away when the God of peace sanctifies us wholly (I Thess. 5:23). Our natural self must be controlled and disciplined by regular habits of private prayer, diligent Bible reading, and sacrificial service for Christ. Paul's attitude must ever be ours if we are to live in holiness of heart and conduct: "I keep under my body, and bring it into subjection: lest that by any means, when I have preached to others, I myself should be a castaway" (I Cor. 9:27).

Dr. Samuel Chadwick once told me that even some holiness movements were strewn with the wreckage from undisciplined affinities between the sexes.

A prominent Methodist writer once declared that John Wesley believed in entire sanctification by faith and by getting up at four o'clock in the morning! In other words, the blessing of heart holiness, received by simple faith in Jesus Christ, can be maintained only by a life of prayerful self-denial. Christians of today are in danger of forgetting that vital principle of sanctification.

It has been my sad lot to witness more than one tragedy in the lives of one-time sanctified ministers who failed to "watch and pray" in the hour of subtle temptation.

"Arm me with jealous care,
  As in Thy sight to live,
And oh, Thy servant, Lord, prepare
  A strict account to give."

4. *In the Sardis church there was lack of spiritual vitality.* "Thou hast a name that thou livest, and art dead" (Rev. 3:1).

The Christians at Sardis went through the usual round of religious service, but there was no real heart in their activities. The fervor of deep spirituality had been displaced by the formality of religious motions. A living organism had been suffocated by rigid organization. Church machinery had taken the place of abundant, supernatural life—that life which alone makes the Church of Christ distinct from the world.

Some years ago I witnessed a scene that has etched itself upon my memory. It was at an important Holiness Camp in the USA. Kneeling at the altar of prayer was a minister's wife, sobbing as if her heart was breaking. I was asked by the District Superintendent to give what help I could to this distressed lady. It seemed like sacrilege to listen to the weeping suppliant at the altar. But duty constrained me to draw near.

Between her sobs this minister's wife prayed a prayer which in substance was this: "O Lord, Thou knowest my need. I am simply going through the motions of Christian service week after week. But there is no spiritual vitality in my life. My heart is dry and barren. O Lord, supply the deep need of my heart."

In the searching light of God's Word that lady made the sad discovery that although she had a name to live (she knew the doctrine of holiness quite well), yet she was dead spiritually.

Only the throbbing, vibrant life of the Holy Spirit

in the heart of the Christian can satisfy Christ and
meet the need of the believer himself.

5. *Lack of heat was the defect in the Laodicean
church.* "Thou art neither hot nor cold. So then because thou art lukewarm, I will spue thee out of my
mouth" (Rev. 3:15, 16).

In the city of Laodicea were springs of lukewarm
water. Jesus used them as an illustration of the spiritual condition of His church there. It was a condition
which is prevalent throughout Christendom today.

Open sin has slain its thousands, but lukewarmness
has slain its tens of thousands. Lukewarmness is that
deadly thing that invades the saintliest precincts and
which brings down the mighty from their throne. The
tragedy of lukewarmness is twofold: (1) It often comes
imperceptibly, almost without being noticed. (2) It
produces substitutes for the real things of the Spirit.

To the Laodiceans Jesus said: "Thou knowest not
that thou art . . . poor, and blind, and naked." Samson
went to sleep on the knees of the charming Delilah and
awoke unaware that his God-given power had departed
from him.

"I will go out as at other times before, and shake
myself. But he wist not that the Lord was departed
from him" (Judges 16:20). All that Samson could do in
that tragic hour was to shake himself. He had lost
the power to shake the Philistines!

There is no sadder sight on earth than that of a
one-time Spirit-anointed preacher who has lost the
unction from heaven but who still goes on preaching.
The same phraseology is there, the same gestures and
intonation. But the warmth and glow of the Holy Spirit
are sadly missing. Some people in the audience may be
deceived by the play-acting. But the discerning saints
realize in their hearts that the glory has departed.

It was said by God of Ephraim that "gray hairs are here and there upon him, yet he knoweth not" (Hos. 7:9).

The members of the Laodicean church had substitutes for true spirituality. Hence their complacent exclamation: "I am rich, and increased with goods, and have need of nothing."

It is ever thus with the lukewarm Christian. Instead of prayer there is talk; instead of love for Christ there is zeal for a cause; instead of discernment of spirit there is mere censoriousness; instead of tenderness of heart there is just human sentiment; instead of true catholicity of spirit there is the spirit of compromise and appeasement.

But the wonder of Christ's address to the Laodicean church is that He makes His most glorious promises to these lukewarm believers. Not only does He solemnly warn them of the awful consequences of their tepid condition. He also pleads with the gentle passion of a Lover: "As many as I love, I rebuke and chasten: be zealous therefore, and repent."

What an amazing offer Christ makes to this church: "I counsel thee to buy of me gold tried in the fire, that thou mayest be rich; and white raiment, that thou mayest be clothed; and anoint thine eyes with eyesalve, that thou mayest see. . . . To him that overcometh will I grant to sit with me in my throne, even as I also overcame, and am set down with my Father in his throne" (Rev. 3:18–21).

Spiritual wealth, celestial adornment, heavenly vision, and ultimate sovereignty with Christ in the coming age—all this is promised to the repentant Christian who will buy with heaven's currency. It is the coinage of faith and obedience.

So there comes the final admonition to the Laodicean assembly: "He that hath an ear, let him hear what the Spirit saith unto the churches."

CHAPTER EIGHTEEN

Call the Witnesses

THE LATE READER HARRIS, Q.C., was well known
as the founder of the Pentecostal League of Prayer in
Britain. He was also renowned as a brilliant lawyer.
One of his illuminating statements was this: "When
I have a poor case in court, I make a speech; but when
I have a good case, I call the witnesses."

The case for full salvation is so good that we cannot finish this book without calling the witnesses.

Of blameless character and unquestioned reliability,
they give clear testimony of the fulness of the Holy
Spirit as a definite experience of grace subsequent to
conversion.

Our first witness is Oswald Chambers, well known
to the Christian world for his unique messages on the
"deep things of God." This is his personal testimony.

"After I was born again, as a boy, I enjoyed the
presence of Jesus Christ wonderfully, but years passed
before I gave myself up thoroughly to His work.

"Later I was in college, and a servant of God came
there and spoke about the Holy Spirit. I determined
that I would get all that there was going, and I went to
my room and asked God as simply and as definitely as

I could for the baptism of the Holy Spirit, whatever that meant.

"From that day for four years nothing but the over-ruling grace of God and the kindness of friends kept me out of an asylum. God used me during those four years in the conversion of souls, but I had no conscious communion with Him. The Bible was the dullest, most uninteresting book in existence, and my bad motiveness of my nature was terrific. I see now that was God taking me through every ramification of my being by the light of the Holy Spirit and His Word.

"The last three months of that four years things reached a climax. I was getting very, very desperate. I knew no one who had what I wanted. In fact, I did not know what I wanted; but I knew that if what I presently had was all the Christianity there was, the thing was a fraud. Luke 11:13 got hold of me. Had I asked definitely for the Holy Spirit? But how could I possibly ask for the Holy Spirit when I was as bad-motived as I was?

"Then this was borne in on me that I had to claim this gift from God on the testimony of Jesus Christ and testify to it. But the thought came: If you testify and claim the gift of the Holy Spirit on the word of Jesus Christ, God will make it known to those who know you best (and they thought I was an angel!) how bad you are in your heart. I was not willing to be a fool for Jesus Christ's sake.

"Those of you who know the experience know very well how God brings you to the point of utter despair, and I did not care one snap of my fingers for anything on earth but to get out of the state I was in.

"There was a little meeting held in Dunoon; I was surrounded by Christian workers who knew me well. A well-known lady worker was asked to take the after-meeting. She did not speak; she put us all to prayer and then sang, 'Touch me again, Lord.' I felt nothing, but I knew emphatically my time had come. I rose to my feet. I had no feeling, no vision of God, but this sheer, dogged determination to take Him at His word, to put this thing to the final test. I stood up and said that.

"That was bad, but what followed was ten times worse. When I sat down the lady worker, who knew me well and knew me in missions, said so sweetly and with smiling face: 'That is very good of our Brother Chambers; he has done that as an example to the rest of you.'

"It was like having your leg cut off and then a piece cut off higher up. Up I got again, and I said: 'I got up for no one's sake; I got up for my own. This Christianity is either a downright fraud, or I have not gotten hold of the right end of the stick.' And I then and there claimed the gift of the Holy Spirit in dogged committal on Luke 11:13. I had no vision of heaven, no vision of angels; I had nothing. I was dry and empty. Then the verse that came to me during that condition was this: 'You shall receive power after that the Holy Ghost is come upon you.' But I had no power, no realization of God, no witness of the Holy Spirit.

"Two days afterwards I was asked to speak at a meeting. I spoke, as empty and as dry as a trumpet, but forty souls came out to the front. Did I praise God? No, I was terrified and left them and went back; I went to an old servant of God and told him what had happened. What do you think he said to me: 'My dear young fellow, don't you remember claiming on the word of Jesus Christ the Holy Spirit as a gift, and He said that you should receive power after that the Holy Ghost came upon you? That is the power.'

"Like a flash something happened inside me, and
I saw that I had been wanting power in my own fist to
show people and say: 'Look what I have; you see what
I have gotten by putting my all on the altar.'

"If the four years previously were hell on earth
those following have been truly heaven on earth. I do
thank God from the bottom of my heart for this. In
Acts 2:4 it says: 'They were all filled with the Holy
Ghost.' Glory be to God, the last aching abyss of the
human heart is filled to overflowing with the love of
God.

"If you read II Corinthians 4 you see the apostle
Paul's message there: 'For we preach not ourselves,
but Jesus Christ as Lord: and ourselves your servants
for Jesus' sake.' Love is the beginning, love is the middle,
and love is the end. You know what He does when He
comes in. He takes out that old carnal nature root and
branch and ramification, and lives inside. And who do
you think you see afterwards?

> Jesus only, Jesus ever,
> Jesus all in all we sing;
> Saviour, Sanctifier, Healer,
> Glorious Lord and coming King.

"Oh, that the Omnipotent God would grant that
everyone would have stripped from them the veil that
the prince of this world has put on and could see the
marvellous freedom God brings. Not myself, but my
Master; not my introspective self, but Jesus only."

The next in the witness box is Dr. Harry E. Jessop.
From my boyhood days I have known personally
this veteran holiness teacher and writer. Samuel Chadwick called him the successor to Thomas Cook as an
exponent of Scriptural sanctification. For many years
a pastor and convention speaker in Britain, Dr. Jessop

later became president of the Chicago Evangelistic Institute (since renamed Vennard College). Now 80 years of age, he retains a remarkable agility of mind and freshness of spirit.

"From that first moment of the realization of saving grace, I wanted all that God could give me. It was not long before I began to feel that, glorious as my new experience in conversion had been, God was now holding before me something of a deeper nature than that which I already enjoyed.

"While my love for Christ was such that it pained me to know that I had grieved Him, my spiritual life was far from constant and my communion was not sustained. I was conscious of a lack of power in service and of a strange inward conflict which did not seem to be consistent with New Testament standards.

"One day, however, an unexpected thing happened. I met a man whose face shone with something I had never seen before. It was a heavenly radiance betokening a real soul satisfaction and suggesting a deep inward rest. As I looked at him, my heart was filled with an unspeakable longing to have what he possessed. But the longer I looked, the more puzzled I became.

"As he looked at me, he evidently read the longing of my hungry heart, for he startled me with a strange question: 'Brother,' said he, 'have *you* been baptized with the Holy Ghost and with fire?'

"My reply must have sounded simple, but it came from my heart as I answered: 'I don't know what you mean by being baptized with the Holy Ghost and fire, but if that is it that shines out of your face, I want it.'

"He was not long in telling me that the radiance on his countenance was the result of a definite spiritual experience, a baptism with the Holy Spirit. Wesley called it the Second Blessing. 'This,' said my new-found

friend, 'is for *you*, and for every child of God who will
seek it today.'

"He began to give me some simple instructions as
to how I might receive it, showing me the need of a
complete consecration, my entire life with all it reaches
being demanded as a living sacrifice to God. When
that consecration was complete, a simple act of faith
would bring the blessing.

"It is a joy to testify that the consecration was made
and the faith exercised; and, blessed be God, the blessing
came!

"There have been definite results, both immediate
and abiding. The phases have been many. Here, however, I shall mention only three.

"First of all, with this baptism with the Holy Spirit,
there came a consciousness of *deep inward cleansing*.

"A second feature of this experience was a *deep
sense of release*. You will notice that again I am using
that word *deep*, for that is exactly what it was—deeper
down than anything I had before known.

"It seemed to reach the very depths of my being.
Inward bonds were broken and fetters snapped, so
that whereas there had been a measure of bondage to
people, their opinions and views, there was now a
glorious liberty in the service of God and in the doing
of His will.

"A further result of this spiritual baptism has been
a *deep inward illumination*. The light seemed to break
away down in the inner recesses of my being. It was
as though subterranean passages, hitherto dark and
unexplored, had been suddenly lighted up and their
darkness chased out by a divine glory which surged
through them.

"Of the abiding peace, the power for service, the
periods of exultant joy, and so many other glorious ac-
companiments, time forbids me to speak, except to say

that every day the marvel grows as to why the Lord should have been so good to me."

Third in our list of witnesses is James T. Bohi, the well-known gospel singer from southern Iowa.

It was my privilege to hear his personal testimony when working with him in a gospel crusade in British Guiana, July 1964.

"I was converted to Christ when a boy of 14 years. Soon after, I sought earnestly to be filled with the Holy Spirit so that I might live a victorious Christian life.

"Time and again I went to an altar of prayer to claim this coveted 'second blessing.' Because I had done all I was told to do—viz., consecrate myself fully to God—I supposed that I had received the sanctifying power of the Holy Spirit. But when my feelings changed, as they did after leaving the altar, I would give in to doubt and unbelief and declare that I did not have the experience of entire sanctification.

"For eighteen months I struggled. I did not fight against the doctrine of Bible holiness; rather did I seek with a longing heart to be fully possessed by the Holy Ghost. At various camp meetings, holiness conventions, and revivals at my local church, I went forward to the altar. But through doubt and fear the blessing eluded me.

"Then came a never-to-be-forgotten summer's afternoon in July. I was out in the fields cultivating soya beans with a tractor and cultivator. For days previously I had been sad and discouraged because of my lack of entire sanctification. In deep depression of spirit I regarded myself as a failure in the Christian life.

"Suddenly the voice of the Holy Spirit came to me with penetrating clarity: 'You can have it today.'

"I tried to reason with God. Here I was, alone in a field with nobody to pray with me. Had I not failed to get through to the blessing even when surrounded by praying friends who did their best to help me? How, then, could I get through when all alone in a field? Thus I reasoned. But the voice of God kept ringing in my ears: 'You can have it today.'

"At last, with a hungry, desperate heart, I stepped off the tractor and knelt beside the cultivator, using it as an altar of prayer.

"It was then about 2:30 p.m. In my mind I said, 'I'll stay here until darkness comes' (when I knew somebody would be looking for me). I fully thought it would take hours of prayer to get through to God for the blessing.

"With a breaking heart I commenced to pray, sobbing out my intense desire to be filled with the Spirit. I don't remember how long I prayed; to me it seemed only five to ten minutes. Suddenly an uncontrollable emotion swept over me. I knew I wanted the experience of heart holiness more than life itself. Then, oh glorious moment! I realized that the blessed Holy Spirit had come into my heart in sanctifying fulness.

"I literally felt His cleansing, energizing power. I was possessed with the greatest joy I had ever known. It was the joy of full salvation. It was a second heaven to me.

"That rendezvous with the Holy Spirit in a farmer's field revolutionized my Christian life. Along with cleansing and rapturous joy came a power for service which hitherto I had lacked.

"Mine is now the privilege of singing the songs of Zion at home and abroad."

Our next witness is Mrs. Louise R. Chapman.

This saintly and talented woman spent twenty years as a missionary in Africa. Then she served as president of the Nazarene Foreign Missionary Society. My own heart has been deeply moved and challenged when listening to the impassioned words of Louise Robinson Chapman. To her has come the fulfilment of the promise of God in the latter days: "I will pour out of my Spirit upon all flesh: and your . . . daughters shall prophesy" (Acts 2:17). Here is her testimony.

"I heard about a second blessing—the promise of the Father. Cleansing from inward pollution, power for victorious life and service, seemed proper and good for me. I claimed the promise and tried to believe, but since I was so happy in my new-found joy, I felt no inward need and obtained no definite experience.

"After some time I began to feel a great soul hunger. I was not free. I knew I needed what Peter received at Pentecost. I longed for the fulness of the blessing.

"I sought heart holiness, publicly and privately, for two years. I prayed in the pasture by day and in my room at night. I spent hours on a nearby mountain alone with God. I asked prayers from my pastor, my teachers, and my friends. Every time the Spirit of God manifested himself in special blessing upon God's people my heart would again cry out for its own need. I began to wonder if there really was a definite experience of heart holiness. I was most miserable.

"Three things troubled me. I still wanted to follow the plans I had made for my own life. I was afraid God wanted me to preach, and I was afraid God was going to send me to Africa as a missionary. If I had been sure God was calling me I would have cast aside my own plans. I didn't like to see or hear women preach. I thought it was dangerous enough for a man to be a holiness preacher, to say nothing of a woman. I thought it would be certain starvation. But worst of all was Africa.

"One noon hour, after weeks of wrestling with God,

I decided to find out once for all what God wanted me
to do. I went into a classroom and locked the door. I
told the Lord why I had come and that I did not intend
to leave until this question was forever settled. I began with my life's plans. I promised God that I would
work no more on them unless I had direct orders
from the Almighty to do so. I decided that it would
be no more painful to starve to death as a despised
woman preacher than to perish of famine in my soul.
I was so hungry after more of God that life meant
little to me if I could not be satisfied.

"Then Africa loomed up. It was not enough to
preach in America—I must preach in Africa. I saw
myself away out in the jungle. I was dressed in a
hideous black dress that began at my ankles and reached
to my fingers and ears. My hair was pulled straight
back and pinned in a little tight knob at the top of
my head. All my teeth except two or three were gone.
I sat on an old soapbox by the side of a grass hut while
a few naked children played at my feet. I started up
in fear, and then I heard myself saying, 'Lord, God
Almighty, You have a little old woman on Your hands
from this very moment; now, and throughout eternity.'

"I had scarcely finished the sentence when something like a great weight slipped off me and went
splashing down into space. I jumped to my feet, feeling as light as a feather. The room seemed to be on
fire with the presence of God. Fear and hunger had
gone and I was free and satisfied. My heart was aflame
with the love of God. I loved His will for me. I was
ready to start immediately for Africa. I had not only
settled my call but had been baptized with the Holy
Ghost.

"So wonderful was the work done in my heart that
day that not once through the years has it ever been
suggested that God did not really baptize me with His

Spirit and completely cleanse and sanctify my soul. Thank God for the gift of the Holy Ghost!"

The fifth witness is H. Kenneth Bedwell.

This eminent missionary and talented Bible college principal is one of my close friends. In the year 1928–1929 we were members of a team of young evangelists who trekked up and down England and Wales for 14 months. Kenneth Bedwell was then the "baby" of the party. Today he is acknowledged to be one of Africa's finest missionaries and convention speakers. He is now in charge of the Nazarene Bible School in Stegi, Swaziland, where hundreds of natives have been trained for full-time ministry to their own people. Brother Bedwell's testimony is this:

"As a youth of nineteen in the village of Whitby, Yorkshire, England, I faced a great crisis. What happened then changed my whole life. From being a defeated and disappointed Christian, I suddenly became a joyous, eager, and victorious worker for Christ. Instead of pursuing my ambition to become a marine engineer, I gave up my job, joined the Holiness Trekkers—a band of five young men dedicated to preaching the gospel up and down Britain—as a prelude to my ultimate purpose of going to Africa as a missionary.

"What is the difference? The answer is simple. God sanctified me wholly and filled me with the Holy Spirit. I experienced what John Wesley designated the 'Second Blessing, properly so called.' The terms may differ, but the blessing is the same.

"It happened like this. For months my heart had been hungry for God and for holiness of heart and life. My Christian life was a failure.

"For several weeks I wrestled and struggled in prayer from early morning until late at night, day after day. But to no avail. Nothing happened. In my stupidity I thought something startling would happen, like the firing of a cannon, and all would be well. I thought that I could persuade God to give me this blessing if only I prayed long enough and loud enough. Two things hindered me—my selfish ambition and my spiritual pride. I wanted God on my own terms and I was not willing to humble myself and confess my need. The struggle went on and victory only receded.

"Then one day I went to a missionary meeting. After the missionary had spoken, Dr. H. E. Jessop preached. His text was, 'The very God of peace sanctify you wholly.' It was just for me! I could hardly wait until the speaker had finished. Immediately I stood to my feet and told the people that I needed this blessing and was ready to surrender all to God.

"While I was still speaking, the fire of God fell upon me and I was filled with the Holy Spirit. My heart was cleansed from inward sin, and that same night God called me to Africa.

"It is thirty-six years since that happened, but the wonderful peace that filled my heart then still abides and grows wider and deeper with the passing of time.

"Looking back over these many years, thirty-three of them spent in Africa, I shall ever thank God for that glorious day. What really did happen?

"Well, first of all, defeat was turned into victory. Where I had been cowardly, God gave me courage; where secret sin defeated me, God gave deliverance.

"Then, secondly, God's will became my will. Instead of seeking my own ways, I was ready to go God's way. The Holy Spirit took control of my life and He still rules there. I was delivered from disobedience and rebellion.

"Thirdly, a new life of inward communion began. Prayer became a delight and the Bible a living book.

"Fourthly, a new passion for souls burned in my

heart which thrust me out into evangelistic work in Britain within a few months, and ultimately to Africa.

"Finally, from that hour there began a life of fruitfulness in service which continues to this day. It has been a joy to see the Spirit of God poured out again and again on the needy folk of this dark continent, and to see many, many of these African people delivered from witchcraft, demon-possession and awful sin and go on to enter into the self-same experience of His fulness; then to lead their own people to enjoy it too.

"These thirty-three glorious years in Africa would never have been possible had not God's Spirit filled me with himself that day."

Our sixth witness is Dr. Charles Ewing Brown, who served successfully as pastor in several large churches in the USA. Dr. Brown also edited the *Gospel Trumpet* and lectured in theology in the Anderson Seminary.

"There came a swift, miraculous spiritual summer to our community in which my infidel, drunken father was converted. I followed him in a few days; some months later my mother entered into the fellowship of the faith.

"Our spiritual leader did not tarry long. He taught the doctrine of entire sanctification. I began to pray earnestly and seek for that blessing. I felt such a burden of yearning on my heart that I can remember it yet as a pain, a longing, a cry to God. I fasted for some time.

"The greatest trouble I had in seeking sanctification was what I found later to be the major infirmity of the modern soul—doubt. No scientist in his laboratory, or scholar in his study, has ever pressed closer to the chilling doubt of the reality of the spiritual life than I pressed as I knelt on the ground amid the awakening grass and the budding flowers, while I sought to see

the throne of the Eternal in the bushes as Moses found
it so many years ago.

"Down on my knees in the orchard at the foot of
the hill, in an agony of yearning desire and struggle
with doubt, I pressed along the road trampled by
Elijah when he heard the strong wind, but God was
not in the wind. He felt a mighty earthquake, but
God was not in the earthquake. After the earthquake,
a fire, but the Lord was not in the fire. And after
the fire, a still, small voice.

"There in the silence, with only the winds rustling
the grass and the trees, the thunders of eternity came
to me from the distance as a soft whisper of God:

" 'It is done. This is Pentecost. This is the baptism
of the Holy Spirit. This is fire and lightning and healing
power. This is heart purity. This is fellowship with
the gentle Jesus, the country Preacher who loved
children; and this is the call to go and minister the
healing of His word and works wherever you can help
others.'

"It has been a long time since I heard the whisper
of Jesus in the old orchard on the hillside. Since then
the days have stretched into years, and the years have
passed into decades, and I have carried His healing
message to men of nearly every race and kind."

My good friend, Dr. Paul S. Rees, has wisely observed that "a Christianity so humble that it does
not testify is false to the New Testament." Therefore
it is a plain duty, as well as a privilege, to add my
own testimony to those witnesses who have just told
us of their experience of the Holy Spirit.

Reared in a godly home, I was soundly converted
to Christ at the age of 13. The new life in Jesus brought
deliverance from those outward sins which had fettered
me.

Further, it brought a peace and joy I had never known before. "Old things have passed away, behold, all things have become new."

Still, not many months elapsed before I realized my need of a further work of grace. A conscious lack of power to witness for Christ at all times, along with wrong tempers and a sense of inner uncleanness, marred my usefulness in the Lord.

But I was privileged to hear the message of full deliverance through the baptism of the Holy Spirit. Such a clear teaching of Bible holiness was amply verified by the radiantly victorious lives of the saints at the little church I attended. My own mother and a humble coal miner were among those convincing witnesses.

After a long struggle, I came to the place of abandonment to God. More than anything else in the world I longed to be filled with His sanctifying Spirit. The climax came during an Easter Convention in London. Twice, in that convention, I went to an altar of prayer, resolved at all cost to obtain the coveted blessing. Relying too much on emotional surges as an evidence of the Spirit's indwelling fulness, I almost missed my Pentecost.

Then God sent a Manchester business man to deal with me as, in desperation, I knelt at the altar. Gently, but firmly, he said to me, "What you need is faith, *not in your own faith* but faith in God." That timely word was a veritable Joshua to lead me into Canaan that Easter Monday.

In simple faith I claimed the promised Holy Spirit. And, according to Galatians 3:14, "that we might receive the promise of the Spirit through *faith*," the Comforter came into my longing heart.

I did not hear a sound as of a rushing mighty wind. Neither did a cloven tongue of fire rest upon my head. Nor was it given me to speak in another language when the Holy Spirit came in.

But my Christian life was revolutionized from that glad hour. Carnal fear was cast out by perfect love. Frustration was exchanged for a life of victory in the Holy Spirit. Prayer became an intense delight and the Bible was my veritable meat and drink.

More wonderful than all was the unveiling of Christ to my longing heart. He became the loadstone of my affections; His beauty and grace ravished my happy soul. To tell of Him to others now became the one business of life. And something happened I had never known before—the Holy Spirit melted me to tears when praying for needy humanity. Truly, the love of God had been shed abroad in my heart by the Holy Ghost (Rom. 5:5).

Many years have passed since that memorable Easter Convention. And those passing years have showed me my native frailty and unworthiness. But they have also brought with them an ever-increasing dependence upon Him who is indeed "the altogether lovely One" and the "chiefest among ten thousand" to my soul.

Conclusion

We have purposely given the testimonies of those Christians who, when they were filled with the Holy Spirit, did not speak with other tongues. This is not meant as an attack upon the present-day Pentecostal Movement. Far from it.

I have some good friends among the Pentecostal brethren, and occasionally I have the privilege of preaching full salvation in their churches. In fact, I admire their evangelistic fervor and devotion to Christ.

But to please God, I must ever walk in the light He has given me after many years of heart-searching and prayerful study of the Scriptures.

So I take my stand on the "more excellent way" of perfect love. For this indeed is the hall-mark of a Spirit-filled life. Without it all the gifts are worthless.

The increasing manifestation of the glossolalia among Christians all over the world is not so much a sign to believers that they are Spirit-filled (Paul plainly stated that "tongues are for a sign, *not* to them that believe, but to them that believe not."—I Cor. 14: 22); rather, it is one of God's mysterious signs that world-wide judgments are about to fall from heaven upon apostate humanity. Diverse languages at the Tower of Babel were God's judgment on the proud builders.

The speaking in other tongues on the Day of Pentecost was followed, not many years later, by awful judgment upon Christ-rejecting Jewry.

Before the bloody French revolution in the 18th century, many Huguenots on the European continent spoke in other tongues.

The present world-wide outburst of the charismatic gifts is a sure sign that universal judgment is soon to fall. The "great and terrible day of the Lord" is at hand.

Let us then not quarrel about speaking in tongues as the initial evidence of the baptism in the Holy Spirit. The most ardent Pentecostalist must admit that a person can speak in tongues even when his heart is carnal. The tragedy of the Corinthian believers is proof of this. But it is impossible for a Christian to be truly *filled* with the Holy Spirit and at the same time be carnal. The very thought of carnality, which is enmity against God (Rom. 8:7), coexisting with the Holy Spirit's fulness in the heart is a libel upon the character and power of the third person of the Godhead!

Rather let us major on the infallible evidence of a Spirit-baptized life—"love out of a pure heart." For this is the end of the commandment (I Tim. 1:5).

Gifts in themselves, no matter how wonderful they may be, can never satisfy the deep longing of the heart. Nor can the glossolalia break down the barriers which alienate a perishing world from God. The all-conquering dynamic is the love of God shed abroad in the heart by the Holy Ghost.

Shall we not bow in obedience and faith before an all-wise and almighty Holy Spirit? Let Him distribute the gifts according to His sovereign will. But let our insistent plea be this:

> "Less than *Thyself*, Oh, do not give,
> In might *Thyself* within me live,
> Come, all thou hast and art."

In response to such a prayer of faith the Comforter, who is the Holy Spirit, will come. Then will He

> "Enlarge, inflame, and fill our hearts
> With boundless charity divine."

Then indeed

> "Shall we all our strength exert,
> And love them with a zeal like Thine,
> And point them to Thy open side,
> The sheep for whom the Shepherd died."

The Holy Spirit alone can fit us for the dying hours of this age. He is the Father's coronation gift to His beloved Son Jesus (Acts 2:33).

He is now Christ's Vicar on earth, and He is pledged to glorify the Lamb of God. This He is doing, and will continue to do, through humble, sanctified Christians on earth.

No matter how deep may be our longing to be filled with the Holy Spirit, His yearning to meet our need is infinitely deeper.

Blessed truth indeed!